SLOBODAN MILOSEVIC'S

YUGOSLAVIA

KIMBERLY L. SULLIVAN

 TWENTY-FIRST CENTURY BOOKS | MINNEAPOLIS

Consultant: Jelena Stewart: BS, University of Belgrade; PhD, Rockefeller
University

*The image on page 1 shows Slobodan Milosevic addressing Serbia's ruling
Socialist Party in Belgrade after he was elected party president in 1992.*

Twenty-First Century Books
A division of Lerner Publishing Group, Inc.
241 First Avenue North
Minneapolis, MN 55401 U.S.A.

Website address: www.lernerbooks.com

Library of Congress Cataloging-in-Publication Data

Sullivan, Kimberly L.
    Slobodan Milosevic's Yugoslavia / by Kimberly L. Sullivan.
        p.   cm. — (Dictatorships)
    Includes bibliographical references and index.
    ISBN 978-0-8225-9098-9 (lib. bdg. : alk. paper)
        1. Yugoslavia—Politics and government—1992–2003—Juvenile literature.
    2. Yugoslavia—Social conditions—Juvenile literature. 3. Milošević,
    Slobodan, 1941–2006—Juvenile literature. I. Title.
    DR1318.S85 2010
    949.703092—dc22   2008053304

Manufactured in the United States of America
1 2 3 4 5 6 – DP – 15 14 13 12 11 10

CONTENTS

BITTER END

ON MARCH 11, 2006, SLOBODAN MILOSEVIC was found dead in his prison cell. Milosevic had served as the president of Yugoslavia from 1997 to 2000. Before that, he had served as president of Serbia, one of Yugoslavia's six republics. At the time of his death, Milosevic was imprisoned in a United Nations (UN) detention center at The Hague, Netherlands. The United Nations is an international peace-keeping and human rights organization. Its detention center in the Netherlands holds people accused of war crimes, or military violations of the international rules of warfare. Milosevic had been imprisoned at The Hague since 2001.

At the time of Milosevic's death, he was on trial for committing war crimes during bloody conflicts in Kosovo, Croatia, and Bosnia-Herzegovina. These regions had all once been part of Yugoslavia, a country in southeastern Europe. The wars occurred as this former

FORMER YUGOSLAVIAN PRESIDENT SLOBODAN MILOSEVIC SITS IN THE courtroom of the United Nations criminal tribunal for the former Yugoslavia on the second day of his trial in February 2002. The UN charged Milosevic with war crimes committed during conflicts between former Yugoslavian regions.

Communist nation had begun to split apart in the 1990s. Milosevic's alleged war crimes included forcing hundreds of thousands of people from their homes and overseeing genocide, or the intentional slaughter of an ethnic or religious group.

Before Milosevic began his defense at The Hague (which he chose to handle himself), prosecutors in the case had spent two years presenting massive amounts of evidence against him, including testimony from witnesses who had survived the wars—among the most brutal in modern European history. Milosevic's death in 2006 meant that the case could not be concluded. An official verdict about his guilt or innocence was never reached.

During Milosevic's trial and even after his death, many supporters stood by Milosevic. They argued that the crimes of which he had

SEVERAL HUNDRED SUPPORTERS OF MILOSEVIC GATHER IN BELGRADE,
Serbia, in June 2004 to protest the anniversary of his removal to The Hague.

been accused either were exaggerated or that he had played no part in them at all. The international community, however, largely condemns Milosevic as a brutal dictator who ruthlessly grabbed power in Serbia and Yugoslavia, suppressed citizens' freedoms and human rights, stirred up hatreds among ethnic groups, and sanctioned genocide and other war crimes. To understand Milosevic's crimes, it is necessary to understand Yugoslavia, a diverse and troubled nation that officially existed from 1918 to 1991.

HISTORIC

THE FORMER YUGOSLAVIA WAS LOCATED in Eastern Europe on the Balkan Peninsula. This peninsula (a body of land surrounded on three sides by water) gets its name from the Balkan Mountains that run through its center. The peninsula is bordered by the Black Sea to the east, the Adriatic Sea to the west, Austria and Hungary to the north, and the Mediterranean Sea to the south. The entire region is commonly referred to as the Balkans. In addition to the former Yugoslavia, the Balkan Peninsula is home to the nations of Romania, Bulgaria, Albania, Greece, and part of Turkey.

The land of the Balkan Peninsula is diverse and beautiful, with seacoasts, majestic mountain ranges, and plains that are ideal for farming. The climate is varied, with cold, snowy winters in the north and in mountainous regions, and hotter, drier weather in the south.

vineyards along the Yugoslavian
coast on the Adriatic Sea.

EARLY PEOPLES

Groups of hunter-gatherers
lived in the Balkan region
thousands of years ago. These
people got their food by hunt-
ing animals and gathering wild
plants. They eventually lived a
more settled life. They took up
farming and herded cattle.

About A.D. 148, the Roman
Empire, based in Italy across

the Adriatic Sea to the west, conquered the Balkan Peninsula. The Romans spread their culture and architecture throughout the region.

Eventually, the power of Rome weakened, and around A.D. 600, new conquerors made their way to the Balkans. These conquerors were Slavs, who came from what are now Poland and Ukraine to the north. The Slavs who conquered the Balkans, called South Slavs, evolved into many ethnic groups, including Serbs, Croats, Slovenes, Macedonians, and others. These ethnic groups formed various nations, and over time, they fought one another—and frequently fought outsiders.

In their early history, the South Slavs practiced a variety of ancient religions. But in the 800s, many South Slavs converted to Christianity, a religion based on the teachings of Jesus Christ and founded in the ancient Middle East. In 1054 the Christian Church split into two halves: the Eastern Orthodox Church (based in what is now Turkey) and the Roman Catholic Church (based in Rome). Some South Slavs affiliated with the Eastern Orthodox Church, while others became Catholic.

In the 1300s, the Ottoman Empire, based in Turkey, began to invade the Balkan nations to expand its territory. Following many bloody and brutal battles, the Ottomans were victorious in many parts of the Balkans. Their conquest had an important impact on the region's religious future. The Ottomans practiced Islam—a religion founded on the Arabian Peninsula in the 600s—and they brought their faith with them to conquered lands. Ottoman rulers allowed Balkan residents to continue practicing Christianity, and many did. But some residents found that converting to Islam—the religion of their rulers—offered them economic and social advantages. Thus the region became split between three main religious faiths: Islam, Eastern Orthodox Christianity, and Roman Catholicism.

By the 1800s, the Ottoman Empire had begun to weaken. Late in the century, several Balkan nations won independence from the

Ottomans. In the early 1900s, the neighboring nations of Serbia, Montenegro, Greece, and Bulgaria banded together to create the Balkan League. The first test of their united power came in 1912. The league wanted to free more Balkan territory from Ottoman control. That year the league fought the First Balkan War against the Ottoman Empire. With Russia's help, the Balkan countries succeeded in winning back land from the Ottomans.

War continued for several more months—only this time fighting was among the Balkan countries themselves. Bulgaria objected to the way the newly acquired territory had been divided, so, in a conflict called the Second Balkan War, it attacked Serbia. Soon, Romania, Greece, and the Ottomans joined Serbia and defeated Bulgaria. By August 1913, the Balkan Wars were over, but thousands were dead and many thousands more had been left homeless as a result of the fighting.

VICTORIOUS BULGARIAN TROOPS IN THEIR CAMP AFTER WINNING THE FIRST
Balkan War in 1913. Serbia and Montenegro (both later part of Yugoslavia) also fought in this war.

WORLD WAR

The smoke had barely cleared from the Balkan Wars when Europe became the battlefield for another major conflict, World War I (1914–1918). The spark that started the war occurred in the city of Sarajevo in Bosnia-Herzegovina in 1914. At this time, Bosnia-Herzegovina was part of the Austro-Hungarian Empire to the north. The archduke Franz Ferdinand, heir to the Austro-Hungarian throne, was visiting the city when he was assassinated. His killer was a member of a Serbian group that wanted to free Bosnia-Herzegovina from Austro-Hungarian control.

The assassination spurred Austria-Hungary to insist that its police officers be allowed access to Serbia to track down the archduke's murderer. Serbia refused Austria-Hungary's demand. Relations between the two countries had been strained for many years, and this incident was the last straw. On July 28, 1914, Austria-Hungary declared war against Serbia.

Across Europe, nations took sides in the war based on historical alliances and treaties. Germany, Bulgaria, and the Ottoman Empire sided with Austria-Hungary. This group became known as the Central powers. On the other side, Russia, Great Britain, France, and Italy (and later the United States) sided with Serbia. This group was known as the Allies. Serbia fell to the Central powers in 1915 but was not out of the fight. The country's remaining soldiers joined other Allied armies and continued to battle.

The idea for a unified nation of Slavs first emerged during World War I. Leaders from Serbia and surrounding countries wanted to create one country that would unite all the South Slavs, or Yugoslavs. With the Declaration of Corfu, finalized on July 20, 1917,

South Slav leaders created a nation of many ethnic groups: Serbs, Croats, Slovenes, Macedonians, Montenegrins, Albanians, and others. Of these, the Serbs comprised the largest ethnic group.

World War I dragged on until November 11, 1918, when the Central and Allied powers signed a truce. A few weeks later, on December 1, 1918, the new South Slav nation became an independent state. Its name was the Kingdom of Serbs, Croats, and Slovenes.

ONE NATION

The Kingdom of Serbs, Croats, and Slovenes occupied the heart of the Balkans, encompassing the modern-day nations of Slovenia, Croatia, Bosnia-Herzegovina, Serbia, Montenegro, and Macedonia. The nation was bordered by the Adriatic Sea on the west; Italy, Austria, and Hungary to the north; Romania and Bulgaria to the east; and Albania and Greece to the south. It measured just under 100,000 square miles (259,000 square kilometers) in area—approximately as big as the U.S. state of Oregon.

National leaders created a Skupstina, or parliament, to make laws for their new kingdom. They also selected a king, Peter Karageorge, a descendant of a Serbian hero who had rebelled against the Ottoman Empire in the early 1800s. Peter had previously governed as the king of Serbia.

Peace in the young nation did not last long. Since there were more Serbs than any other ethnic group in the kingdom, Serbian influence was strong. The nation's capital, Belgrade, was in Serbia. People from other ethnic groups were unhappy with Serbian dominance.

YUGOSLAVIA AND ITS
EUROPEAN NEIGHBORS
(MID-1900s)

In addition, Serbia's citizens were mostly Eastern Orthodox Christian, yet Serbia controlled the region of Kosovo, whose residents (called Kosovars) were primarily Muslims, or followers of Islam. The Kosovars wanted independence from the rest of Serbia because they resented being governed by Christians. Many Serbs, however, saw Kosovo as part of their ethnic heritage and were unwilling to let the territory go.

Into the 1920s, tensions continued to mount in the Kingdom of Serbs, Croats, and Slovenes. With the country teetering on the brink of civil war, the nation's second king, Alexander, dismissed parliament and seized all control for himself. He ruled as a dictator—a leader with absolute power.

In 1929 King Alexander renamed his kingdom Yugoslavia (Land of the South Slavs). He managed to quiet the ethnic unrest for several years and created a national constitution in 1931. A

Macedonian revolutionary assassinated Alexander in 1934. The king left behind one son, Peter, who at the age of eleven was too young to rule.

Two men stepped in to lead the nation. Alexander's cousin Prince Paul took the throne, while Milan Stojadinovic served as prime minister and oversaw the day-to-day running of government. Stojadinovic became friendly with Adolf Hitler, the Nazi dictator in Germany, and Benito Mussolini, the Fascist dictator in Italy.

KING ALEXANDER AND HIS SON, Prince Peter, pose for a photo in 1931. Alexander was assassinated in 1934.

Both Hitler and Mussolini were Fascist dictators. In a Fascist system, the government has complete control over a nation's politics, culture, society, and economy. Germany and Italy made a treaty with Japan in 1940, and the three nations became known as the Axis powers.

MORE WAR

World War II (1939–1945) officially began on September 1, 1939, when Germany invaded Poland. Germany pressured Prince Paul to side with the Axis powers during the war, and against the wishes of many

Yugoslavians, Prince Paul agreed. The Axis fought the Allied powers, led by France, Britain, the Soviet Union, and later the United States.

Supporting the Axis turned out to be Prince Paul's biggest mistake. Many members of Yugoslavia's military supported the Allies, and they joined with the British to overthrow Paul's government. Peter, the son of Yugoslavia's assassinated King Alexander, was by then seventeen. Although still very young, he took the throne and announced that Yugoslavia would be neutral in the war.

Declaring its neutrality did not save Yugoslavia from warfare. Germany attacked Yugoslavia in 1941 and conquered its army in just a few days. While the Yugoslavian military was weak in the face of the powerful German war machine, the country's citizens managed to launch a fierce opposition. They created a number of resistance groups to fight against the occupying German forces.

One of the largest resistance organizations was the Yugoslav National Liberation Army, led by a Croatian man named Josip Broz, also called Josip Broz Tito. The group was organized around a Communist philosophy.

JOSIP BROZ TITO, SHOWN HERE with his dog in June 1944, was the leader of the Yugoslav National Liberation Army during World War II. Tito was from Croatia.

YUGOSLAVIAN RESISTANCE MOVEMENTS

Yugoslavia's opposition to German occupation during World War II was fierce. Across the country, resistance groups fought the Germans using any weapons available. The two largest opposition groups were the Chetniks and the Yugoslav National Liberation Army. The Chetniks were primarily Serbs who supported the old Yugoslavian monarchy (rule by kings and queens). The National Liberation Army was led by Communist leader Josip Broz Tito. Members of the National Liberation Army, also called Partisans, supported the creation of a new Communist government for Yugoslavia rather than continuation of the old Yugoslavian monarchy.

While Yugoslavian resistance fighters fought fiercely against the Germans, the German invaders were equally fierce. They were brutal in their efforts to subdue the Yugoslavian resistance. One horrifying incident occurred near Slobodan Milosevic's hometown of Pozarevac, Serbia. In their 1999 book *Milosevic: Portrait of a Tyrant*, authors Dusko Doder and Louise Branson elaborate: "When a handful of German soldiers lost their lives in a battle with the Partisans, the Nazis went into a high school in a town not far from Pozarevac and machine-gunned all the students and their teachers in the school yard."

Communism is a political and economic system in which, in theory, all members of society share equally in a nation's wealth and resources. Under Communism, the government controls all business and the economy. Private enterprise is not allowed. The Soviet Union, with political power centered in Russia, had set up a Communist government in 1917. Many people around the world, including Tito and his followers, were attracted to Communism with its promise of economic equality.

Throughout World War II, Tito's popularity grew. He developed good relations with the Allied forces. When they defeated the Axis powers in 1945, Tito took the reins of the new Yugoslavian government. He first took the title marshal and later became president.

SOCIALISM AND COMMUNISM

Starting with the Soviet Union in 1917, many nations set up Communist governments in the early part of the twentieth century. These governments called themselves Communist, but actually they ran according to the principles of Socialism. Communism and Socialism are very similar, and the terms are often used interchangeably. The principles behind both systems stem from the work of nineteenth-century German political philosophers Karl Marx and Friedrich Engels.

In a famous book called *The Communist Manifesto* (1848), Marx and Engels wrote about the "means of production." By this term, they meant the tools and facilities for making goods, such as factories. In a Socialist system, the government (which represents all the people) owns the means of production. Citizens work at government-owned industries, and together all citizens enjoy the profits that their labor produces. The profits do not go to a private business owner but instead go to society as a whole.

Marx and Engels described Socialism as a necessary step along the road to Communism. Under a Communist system, Marx and Engels wrote, there would be no need for government. People would choose to work at the jobs they preferred, and the combined labor of the entire society would provide enough goods for everyone to have what they needed. Marx and Engels believed that Communism would lead to a utopian, or perfect, society.

In the twenty-first century, the Soviet Union no longer exists, and many other nations have abandoned their Communist governments. But China, Cuba, and some other countries are still so-called Communist nations. Actually, these nations are really Socialist societies that have the goal of someday reaching Communism.

COMMUNIST

AS THE LEADER OF POSTWAR YUGOSLAVIA, Josip Broz Tito had a massive task ahead of him. More than one million Yugoslavs had been killed during World War II, and the nation's largest city and capital, Belgrade, had been reduced to rubble. The country would face its challenges with a new name, the Federal People's Republic of Yugoslavia, which it adopted in 1946.

The nation consisted of six republics: Bosnia-Herzegovina, Croatia, Macedonia, Montenegro, Serbia, and Slovenia. Two independent provinces, Kosovo and Vojvodina, were located within Serbia. One of Tito's biggest challenges involved keeping this diverse country—with its many ethnic groups—together as a unified whole. Tito projected himself as a man who represented all of Yugoslavia rather than just one small part of it. This reputation served him well and made him popular throughout the country.

THE STREETS AND BUILDINGS IN BELGRADE, YUGOSLAVIA, SUFFERED GREAT damage during World War II.

POWER TO THE PEOPLE

Immediately following World War II, the Soviet Union occupied many nations of Eastern Europe and set up Communist governments there. Tito also set up a Communist government in

AUSTRIA

HUNGARY

SLOVENIA
Ljubljana

CROATIA

VOJVODINA

Y U G O S L A V I A

Belgrade
Pozarevac

BOSNIA-
HERZEGOVINA
Sarajevo

SERBIA

MONTE-
NEGRO

KOSOVO
Racak

ROMANIA

BALKAN MTNS.

BULGARIA

ITALY

Adriatic Sea

ALBANIA

MACEDONIA

GREECE

**YUGOSLAVIA
(1918–1991)**

Miles
0 25 50 75

0   50   100
Kilometers

Yugoslavia, but his brand of Communism was unique. In the Soviet Union, power was concentrated in the hands of the national government. Tito's Communist system, called Titoism, was more flexible. Tito spread power throughout the governments of Yugoslavia's republics and provinces. Thus both the regional- and national-level governments held substantial power. One benefit of this system was that it allowed regional governments to adapt to the differing needs of their diverse ethnic and religious groups. On the negative side, the system also led to widening gaps among the republics and provinces, as each sought policies suited to the unique preferences of its own people.

Tito based his Communist system on the writings of Karl Marx and Friedrich Engels, nineteenth-century German philosophers who are considered the fathers of Communist thinking. Marx and Engels supported a Communist government that would be run by the working people. The point was to allow the people to govern themselves and be their own employers. From this theory, the Yugoslavian system of Communist self-management was born. At

A COUNTRY OF MANY NATIONS

Yugoslavia was home to many different ethnic groups—Serbs, Croats, Slovenes, Albanians, and others—and these groups did not always agree on important political issues. Each of the nation's republics and provinces had one or two dominant ethnic groups, as well as minority ethnic groups. For example, in Serbia as a whole, Serbs made up the majority of the population. In the Serbian province of Kosovo, however, Albanians were in the majority, while Serbs were a minority group. To complicate matters, different ethnic groups belonged to different religious faiths. For instance, Serbs and Montenegrins were primarily Eastern Orthodox Christians, while Albanians were Muslim, and Croats were Roman Catholic.

Additionally, citizens often have feelings of patriotism for the country in which they live. This was not the case for many people in Yugoslavia. Because their country was new and its people were so diverse, many Yugoslavians did not feel patriotic toward their country as a whole. Instead, many Yugoslavians felt loyalties toward their own republics and ethnic groups. People often identified with and traced their family roots to these places and groups, instead of to the nation as a whole.

the local level, Yugoslavian workers were organized into hundreds of small groups called communes. These groups were in charge of certain small segments of society. For instance, communes oversaw local utilities, such as electrical power and water systems. They also did economic planning, such as determining how much money industrial workers would be paid.

Yugoslavia was also unique in how it dealt with farmland. At first, Tito's government followed the Soviet model. It took farmland out of private hands and set up government-run farms called collectives. But the collectives were inefficient and not able to produce enough food to feed the nation, so Tito disbanded them and gave farmland back to private owners. With farmers back in charge of their own land, agricultural production climbed quickly.

In addition, unlike the Soviet Union and other Communist nations, where the government strictly controlled all economic activities, Tito let the free market, or the forces of private enterprise,

WORKERS PREPARE CANNED MEAT FOR EXPORT AT A FACTORY NEAR
Belgrade, Yugoslavia, in 1964.

determine how many goods would be produced and how much they would cost. In some ways, Tito's system combined the best aspects of Communism and capitalism, or free enterprise.

BEHIND THE SCENES

Tito promoted his unique system of Communism in part so that Yugoslavia did not appear to be too closely allied with the Soviet Union or its powerful leader, the dictator Joseph Stalin. Tito did this because he wanted Yugoslavia also to be an ally of powerful non-Communist nations such as the United States. But since the United States and other non-Communist nations were hostile toward Communist countries—especially the Soviet Union—Yugoslavia had to maintain its independence from the Soviet Union.

Tito's stance angered Joseph Stalin, whose government exercised strict control over the other Communist nations of Eastern Europe. The Soviet Union was not pleased with Yugoslavia's decision to break away from the Soviet brand of Communism, and tension between the two nations persisted for decades.

In some ways, Tito's Yugoslavia was a success. Some Yugoslavians, especially skilled professionals such as doctors and engineers, prospered under the unique combination of Communism and free-market systems. These people spent their money on vacations, new cars, and other luxuries. But Tito's system was not as efficient as a fully capitalist economy. Yugoslavia's economy survived only with the help of loans from foreign nations, including the United States. The majority of citizens in Tito's Yugoslavia did not enjoy a high standard of living.

Although Titoism gave some power to local governments and working people, Tito made certain that he was always holding the reins of control. His government censored the media—monitoring newspapers, radio, and other news outlets and suppressing any antigovernment messages. At the same time, Tito rallied people to support the Communist system with slogans such as "Brotherhood and Unity."

Because Tito wanted Yugoslavians to be loyal to the state instead of to religious institutions, the government discouraged public religious worship, banned some religious groups, and arrested and killed some religious leaders. Tito's political party, the League of Communists of Yugoslavia (LCY), was the nation's only legal political party. In 1963 the Yugoslavian parliament made Tito president for life—thus furthering his hold on power.

A NEW CONSTITUTION

By the early 1970s, Josip Broz Tito had been in control of Yugoslavia for almost three decades. He knew that after his death, the Yugoslavian government might not hold together. To strengthen national government systems, Tito created a new Yugoslavian constitution in 1974.

The 1974 constitution maintained the power-sharing system that had been established after World War II. The Yugoslavian republics of Serbia, Croatia, Bosnia-Herzegovina, Montenegro, Slovenia, and Macedonia and the provinces of Vojvodina and Kosovo each held substantial power on their own, apart from the national government.

The constitution also established an eight-person "collective presidency." Under this system, the presidents of the eight republics and provinces sat together, along with Tito, to make national-level decisions. The collective presidency was assisted in its work by the Federal Executive Council (FEC). The FEC consisted of the heads of the country's twelve major government departments, including the agriculture, finance, foreign affairs, and defense departments, as well as a prime minister, two deputy prime ministers, and other representatives.

TITO, SHOWN HERE WITH HIS WIFE in 1976, created a new constitution in Yugoslavia in the 1970s.

The Skupstina (Federal Assembly) was the national legislature. This body had two chambers, the Federal Chamber and the Chamber of Republics and Provinces. Members of local communes selected Federal Chamber representatives, while legislatures in each republic and province selected representatives to the Chamber of Republics and Provinces.

Each republic and province also had its own government to handle internal matters. The republic and provincial governments were structured much like the national government, with a president and a legislature. The legislatures made laws, while the president oversaw the government and saw to it that laws were enforced.

On its surface, Tito's Yugoslavia looked like a democracy—a government that allows citizens to vote for candidates for many political offices. However, below the surface, Tito's hand was firmly in control. His political party, the LCY, screened all potential political candidates. Only those approved by the party could run for office. So while citizens could vote, their choices were limited to only Communist candidates.

FREE FALL

Tito had hoped that his 1974 constitution would be strong enough to hold Yugoslavia together after his death. But when Tito died on May 4, 1980, the collective presidency became dysfunctional. The eight presidents of the republics and provinces could no longer agree on national matters or work together the way they had under their strong former president. The republics and provinces retained their independence, while the national government in Belgrade was limited in its power.

Meanwhile, the Yugoslavian economy was faltering. Tito's free-market-Communism combination had never fully succeeded. Despite some prosperity, many Yugoslavians lived in poverty and the unemployment rate was on the rise. Loans from the United States and other nations had accumulated quickly, and interest payments mounted. Between 1971 and 1983, Yugoslavia's debt to foreign nations grew from $4 million to $20.5 billion.

At the same time, Eastern Europe's other Communist countries were also suffering economic hardships. The Communist system led by the Soviet Union was collapsing, and Yugoslavia was in a downward spiral with it.

Inflation (rising prices) increased rapidly throughout the country. Consumer goods—everything from coffee and detergent to gas for cars—were in short supply. By the mid-1980s, many Yugoslavians spent the majority of their meager incomes on food. The main unit of Yugoslavian currency, called the dinar, was virtually worthless.

People demanded economic reforms, but the government officials who had been selected and left behind by Tito were all solid Communists. They had lived their lives under the restrictions of the Communist Party and were not enthusiastic about implementing major reforms. If Yugoslavia were to survive, it would need new leadership.

CHAPTER 3

NEW

YUGOSLAVIA WAS IN NEED OF A NEW LEADER after Josip Broz Tito's death, and one emerged. He was a Serbian named Slobodan Milosevic. Historians know very little about Milosevic's childhood. During his time in political office, he destroyed childhood photographs and records, leaving little information for biographers to find. Even his exact birthday is unknown. He was born in August 1941, shortly after Germany invaded Yugoslavia during World War II, but there is confusion as to the precise day. According to one source, he was born on August 22. Another source says August 29, while a third source says only that he was born in August.

Milosevic was born in a small town in eastern Serbia called Pozarevac. Shortly before Slobodan's birth, his parents had moved there from a poor, remote, mountainous region in Montenegro. His

BLOOD

parents divorced after the war, and his father, Svetozar, left Serbia and took a job teaching history at a school in Montenegro. Slobodan and his mother, Stanislava, stayed in Pozarevac. His mother taught school and was active in the Communist Party.

As a boy, Slobodan had fragile health and avoided physical activity, including sports and physical education classes at school. His neighbors remember him as always trying to keep his shoes clean, despite the muddy Pozarevac streets. They also remember that he was a very good student.

Slobodan met Mirjana Markovic in December 1958, when they were in high school together. Neither was popular among the other students, and after they met, they became inseparable sweethearts. They were both good students who won college scholarships to the University of Belgrade.

YOUNG COMMUNIST

Slobodan Milosevic was eighteen years old when he joined the Communist Party at the University of Belgrade. He immediately showed skill at getting other party members to follow his lead. He organized rallies and recruited other students for party work.

Milosevic quickly grasped the importance of working within the rules and structure of the Communist Party. He knew, for example, that if a person showed too much ambition, the party leadership might get nervous and rein in that person's power. He had seen it happen to others, so he was careful to hide his own ambition from party colleagues.

He met Ivan Stambolic when they were both studying law at the university. Ivan's uncle, Peter Stambolic, was a high-ranking Communist Party official, and Ivan dreamed of following in his uncle's footsteps. He and Milosevic quickly became friends.

Milosevic graduated from the University of Belgrade Law School in 1964. He had done well in all his classes, except the one that focused on physical skills and prepared students to serve in the Yugoslavian armed forces.

He had continued to date Mirjana Markovic, and they married on March 14, 1965. (They later had two children, a son, Marko, and a daughter, Marija.) In 1968 he completed his mandatory military service. Early in his professional career, he worked in a variety of positions in the national capital of Belgrade. He served as an economic adviser to the mayor of Belgrade and then as the city's Information Department chief. As head of the Information Department, Milosevic was involved in media censorship—controlling the messages that the government issued to people.

SOCIALISM—THE THEORY

Yugoslavia's government was patterned after the idea of Socialism. Socialism is a political and economic philosophy that promotes the equality of all citizens. In a Socialist society, no one is supposed to be richer or poorer than anyone else. Every person works at a job for which he or she is best suited. In return, every person receives food, clothing, shelter, and other necessities of life.

In a Socialist society, the government owns factories and other businesses. This system prevents a small number of businesspeople from making great fortunes while workers earn very low wages for their labor. When the government (which represents all the people) owns a factory, the factory's profits do not belong to one individual factory owner. Instead, everyone in society shares the profits equally. People who promote Socialism believe that in a Socialist system, employees will want to work hard, so that their places of employment will be successful and everyone will reap the rewards.

German philosophers Karl Marx and Friedrich Engels are recognized as the fathers of modern Socialism. They wrote *The Communist Manifesto* (1848), in which they laid out the foundation for a Socialist revolution. During this revolution, Marx and Engels predicted, people would demand a society in which everyone shared riches rather than allowing them to be hoarded by a select few wealthy individuals. Marx and Engels believed that citizens would be willing to work together to achieve economic success for their country. They argued that Socialism was superior to capitalism—an economic system in which people work at privately owned businesses and earn money to benefit only themselves and their families.

In Yugoslavia's Communist system, people often earned jobs and promotions through party friends and connections. Ivan Stambolic's uncle Peter helped his nephew's political career, and Stambolic in turn helped Milosevic. In the late 1960s, for example, Ivan Stambolic became director of the government-run energy company Technogas. He left in 1972 to lead the Belgrade Chamber of Commerce, and Milosevic took his place at Technogas. By 1975 Stambolic was prime minister of the republic of Serbia, at which time he put Milosevic in charge of Yugoslavia's largest government-run bank, Beobanka.

ETHNIC BREAKDOWN

In 1981 the ethnic groups in Yugoslavia broke down as follows:

Ethnic Group	Percentage of Yugoslavian Population
Serbs	36.0
Croats	19.7
Muslim Slavs	8.9
Slovenes	7.8
Albanians	7.7
Macedonians	6.0
Montenegrins	2.6
Hungarians	1.9
Other	9.4

Milosevic and Stambolic remained close while Milosevic made many other powerful friends. He had the ability to say the right things to people, thereby making a good impression. He managed to build good relationships with the U.S. ambassador to Yugoslavia and with wealthy U.S. businesspeople while also remaining on good terms with Yugoslavia's Communist Party leaders.

ONWARD AND UPWARD

In the early years after Tito's death, Yugoslavia was showing signs of unrest. The six republics and two provinces grew increasingly more hostile to working together at the national level. But Milosevic stayed clear of politics in these years. He kept a low profile while working at Beobanka. He learned and advanced through the world of banking and finance, frequently traveling to the United States and Europe.

In 1982 Ivan Stambolic rose to become the leader of Belgrade's Communist Party. In turn, he selected Milosevic to join the Serbian Communist Party's Executive Committee. The following year, in 1983, Milosevic spoke on behalf of the Communist Party to a gathering of staff members from the popular Yugoslavian newspaper *Politika*.

The newspaper had been a personal favorite of Tito's, and he had given the staff a great deal of freedom from government control. Milosevic told the reporters and editors that the post-Tito Communist Party had new, stricter expectations for the paper. The staff members were not eager to accept party control, however, and at that point, Milosevic did not argue with them.

SOCIALISM—THE REALITY

Karl Marx and Friedrich Engels's theories did not turn into reality in most of the countries that structured their economies on their ideas. In the Soviet Union and the Communist nations of Eastern Europe, the government gave everyone an apartment, a job, and a wage—whether they worked hard or not and whether their workplaces were successful or not. Since hard work did not translate into higher pay or other benefits, employees were not motivated to work harder to make their government-owned factories and other businesses succeed. Business managers were also not as motivated as managers of privately owned enterprises. As a result, factories and other businesses did not run efficiently. The Soviet Union and other Communist nations suffered from all sorts of economic difficulties, ranging from a lack of food and household goods on store shelves to a lower standard of living than people enjoyed in the West (Western Europe and North America).

Ivan Stambolic became leader of the Serbian Communist Party in 1984, and Milosevic accepted the post that Stambolic was leaving behind. Thus Milosevic became Belgrade's new Communist Party leader. In this position, he cracked down on dissidents (those who speak out against the government), including writers. He was no longer lenient with *Politika* and other newspapers. He was a staunch Communist and would not allow the media to promote any ideas that opposed Communist ideals.

Milosevic's wife, Mirjana, was useful in helping him achieve his pro-Communist goals. At the time, Communist ideology was losing its popularity in Yugoslavia's universities. Professors lectured less about Communist ideals and more about liberal, anti-Communist thinking. Mirjana was a university sociologist, and she used her powerful acquaintances and connections in the nation's educational system to help block this change. She encouraged university officials to move the curriculum back to more traditional Communist theory.

On January 25, 1986, Milosevic took over Ivan Stambolic's old job as the leader of the Communist Party of Serbia. He got the job only with a great deal of help from Stambolic and despite the fact that his wife's uncle, Draza Markovic, was one of the candidates competing with him for the position. At the same time, Ivan Stambolic became president of Serbia. The two men were best of friends and seemed to have all Serbia in the palms of their hands.

IVAN STAMBOLIC *(LEFT)* **EMBRACES** Slobodan Milosevic in June 1986. The two friends were powerful allies in Serbian politics in the 1980s.

CHAPTER 4

HOT

IN THE YEARS AFTER TITO'S DEATH, formerly repressed ethnic tensions began bubbling to the surface. The first trouble spot was the province of Kosovo. The province was home to mostly Albanian Muslims, with a small number of Christian Serbs. Between 1971 and 1981, the number of Serbs living in the province had dropped from 18.3 percent to 13.2 percent of the total population. The number of Albanian Muslims had increased.

The changing population stemmed from several factors. First, Albanian Muslims generally had larger families than did Christian Serbs. Also, the Albanian population steadily increased through immigration from neighboring Albania. At the same time, many Christian Serbs fled Kosovo as the Albanian population increased.

Kosovo was technically part of Serbia, although it enjoyed a great deal of independence, including sending its own

ETHNIC ALBANIANS PROTEST IN the streets of Kosovo's capital city of Pristina in the 1980s.

president to the national collective presidency. But Kosovo's Albanians resented Serbian control in their province, and the Kosovo legislature frequently blocked actions initiated by Serbia. As early as 1981, Albanians in Kosovo had begun protesting for greater independence from Serbia. The protests soon grew so violent that the Yugoslavian government sent the national police to stop them. Meanwhile, the long-standing tensions between the Serbs and the Albanian majority ran higher than ever.

While the Albanians clamored for more independence, Serbia's leaders wanted to draw Kosovo under greater Serbian control. When Ivan Stambolic became president of Serbia in 1986, he was quick to express interest in reducing the province's power. Albanian Kosovars protested, demanding that Kosovo become a fully independent republic of Yugoslavia, completely free from ties to Serbia. This time, the government sent the Yugoslavian military to restore order.

The military action did not silence the protests for long. Unemployment was on the rise in Kosovo, and the province's Albanian population was growing increasingly dissatisfied with the political and economic situation. One complicating factor was that most Albanians in Kosovo spoke only Albanian. They did not speak Serbo-Croatian, the dominant language elsewhere in Yugoslavia, so they could not seek work outside Kosovo. They were largely shut out of the Yugoslavian economy and were angry about it.

The Yugoslavian national government stepped in to quiet the Albanian Kosovars' demands for independence. The military group selected to address the problem was the State Security Service. This organization was normally charged with fighting terrorism and serious internal security threats. In this case, it used spies to identify dissidents. According to Leslie Benson, author of *Yugoslavia: A Concise History*, "The severity of the punishment inflicted on the demonstrators, many of them teenagers, stirred up fears . . . . Sentences of 10–15 years in jail were commonplace for those convicted (as they invariably were, once accused) of political offenses or violence against the security forces."

But such heavy-handed tactics were ineffective in dealing with the situation in Kosovo. In fact, the harsh punishments only turned public opinion away from the national government.

Meanwhile, the Serbs in Kosovo argued that they were the victims of Albanian oppression. They claimed that Albanians were forcing them out of Kosovo and suppressing their culture. Several months after Slobodan Milosevic became the leader of Serbia's Communist Party, a copy of an internal memo from the Serbian Academy of Sciences and Arts was made public. The memo voiced strong feelings of discontent among Serbs, as well as claims that Albanians were mistreating Serbs in Kosovo. The memo also charged that with the creation of Yugoslavia, the Serbs had been divided into separate political units and that Tito had helped every group in Yugoslavia except Serbs.

NATIONALIST

The tensions in Kosovo coincided with Slobodan Milosevic's rise to the top of the Serbian Communist Party. They also suited him politically. Milosevic was stubborn and driven to gain power. At the same time, he was a talented politician. He was skilled in appealing to ordinary people and gaining their support. He was traditional and conservative (supportive of established institutions and ways of doing things), which appealed to the older generation of Serbs who were used to strict Communist rule.

Milosevic was a strong supporter of Serb nationalism—the intense loyalty and protectiveness that Serbs felt for their homeland and ethnic identity. He was determined to use his political power to promote the welfare of Serb people, and Serbs loved him for his commitment to them. Milosevic believed that the Serbs—whether they lived in Bosnia-Herzegovina, Kosovo, or Croatia—were a nation of people who should be allowed to remain politically united with other Serbs.

When Milosevic took control of Serbia's Communist Party in 1986, he did not immediately join the fight in Kosovo. Rather than declaring himself a supporter of the Serbs' cause there, he took a more moderate approach at the beginning.

Meanwhile, economic conditions throughout Yugoslavia continued to decline. Workers' incomes dropped sharply throughout the 1980s. To protest for better working conditions, higher pay, and better management, workers frequently went on strike, refusing to work until their demands were met. The number of labor strikes rose during the mid-1980s, soaring from 174 in 1982 to 1,570 in 1987. People were miserable and desperate for someone who could give them hope.

Slobodan Milosevic recognized that old Communist slogans such as "Brotherhood and Unity" no longer worked to motivate and unite citizens. Yugoslavians knew that Socialist economic policies were not helping them. Milosevic needed another way to appeal to his people, and that way was through an appeal to Serb nationalism. By appealing to fellow Serbs, Milosevic was able to increase his power throughout the republic of Serbia as well as in other parts of Yugoslavia.

Yet Milosevic's message appealed only to Serbs. The other ethnic groups, including Croats and Albanians, recognized that Milosevic did not represent them or their interests. Suspicious and fearful of him, they believed that he did not have the best interests of the entire country at heart but instead would do whatever he could to help the Serbs.

POWER HUNGRY

Ivan Stambolic, Milosevic's old friend and political ally, saw the anger brewing between Serbs and Albanians in Kosovo. As president of Serbia, he was moderate in his support of Serbs. He asked Milosevic, the leader of the Serbian Communist Party, to try to calm the Kosovo Serbs, who were becoming violent in their protests.

In April 1987, Milosevic attended a meeting with Communist Party leaders in Kosovo. While he was there, thousands of Serb protesters surrounded the building where the meeting was taking place. The police, who were primarily ethnic Albanians, confronted the protesters and beat them. Then Milosevic came forward to speak to the protesters. He said, "Nobody should dare beat you, no one has the right to beat *you*."

Many historians have pointed to this public incident as evidence that Milosevic overtly favored the Serbs over other ethnic groups in Yugoslavia. The reasoning behind the claim is that he emphasized the final word *you*, suggesting that the Serb protesters were superior to the Albanian police officers who were beating them.

MILOSEVIC, SHOWN HERE AT A press conference in 1990, seemed to side with the Serbs against the Kosovar Albanians in 1987.

Stambolic was not pleased that his old political ally had apparently sided with the Serbs. While Stambolic was unhappy, the Serbs were thrilled that they had a strong supporter at the top level of the Communist Party. Milosevic's popularity among his fellow Serbs soared.

Milosevic boosted his popularity even further by securing control of the media in Serbia and dictating the messages that went out to citizens. Years earlier, as head of the Belgrade Information Department, Milosevic had gathered the contacts and know-how to direct the media to spread his message. This media control guaranteed that Milosevic was seen in the most favorable light and that alternative viewpoints were not presented.

At this point in his political career, Milosevic no longer had any need for his old friend Ivan Stambolic, since Milosevic held enough power on his own to propel his political fortunes. So Milosevic engineered a plan to get rid of him. Milosevic's media contacts began to publish and televise negative stories about Stambolic and a close ally of his, Dragisa Pavlovic. According to media reports, their "crime" was a lack of support for the pro-Serb nationalist anger that was spreading throughout Serbia and other parts of Yugoslavia.

At first Stambolic was completely unaware that Milosevic was behind the attacks. He defended himself and his trusted friend Pavlovic, but Milosevic managed to have Pavlovic removed from his high-level Communist Party position during a Serbian Communist Party meeting on September 23, 1987.

Three months later, in elections held on December 14, 1987, Stambolic—his reputation thoroughly savaged by Milosevic—lost his position as president of Serbia. Milosevic had successfully betrayed and destroyed the political career of the man who had helped him fulfill his own political goals. Only when it was too late

MILOSEVIC MAKES A SPEECH IN BELGRADE IN FEBRUARY 1989. LATER that year, he became president of Serbia.

did Stambolic realize what his old friend had done to him.

With Stambolic out of the way and Milosevic's popularity among Serbs soaring, Milosevic had a perfect opportunity to gather even more political power. On May 8, 1989, voters chose Slobodan Milosevic as president of Serbia.

DEAD END

Ivan Stambolic's suffering did not end after Milosevic betrayed him politically in 1987. Stambolic mysteriously disappeared in 2000, and his dead body was found three years later in a pit in northern Serbia. In 2006 a Serbian court ruled that Milosevic had ordered his former friend's murder.

SHOCK THERAPY

Around this time, Communist governments throughout Eastern Europe were collapsing as citizens demanded more freedom and stronger economies. In late 1989, German citizens tore down the Berlin Wall, which had separated Communist East Germany from democratic West Germany since 1961, and the countries reunited. The Soviet Union was also starting to fall apart, and at about this time, Czechoslovakia removed its Communist leaders in a peaceful process known as the Velvet Revolution.

Since the rest of Communist Eastern Europe was no longer a political or military threat, the United States and other Western nations had less reason to continue their economic support for Yugoslavia. They reduced their loans to the Yugoslavian government, further damaging the country's already troubled economy, which was still burdened by international debt. Previously, Yugoslavia had made money by exporting (selling abroad) goods such as machinery, electrical equipment, and vehicles to various countries. But Yugoslavian exports also declined, and fac-

PEOPLE FROM WEST BERLIN gather at the Berlin Wall on November 12, 1989, as East German guards demolish a section of the wall.

tories shut down, throwing people out of work. Other economic difficulties included soaring unemployment and runaway inflation.

Yet the international community did not want to see Yugoslavia plummet into economic chaos. Two major international financial organizations, the World Bank and the International Monetary Fund, suggested a program called shock therapy to help transform Yugoslavia's economy from Socialism into a more capitalist system.

A key supporter of shock therapy was Ante Markovic, the prime minister of Yugoslavia's FEC. Markovic sought to use free-market forces to improve the economy throughout Yugoslavia. He even expressed the desire for a political system that allowed multiple competing political parties, instead of the old Yugoslavian system that allowed only the Communist Party to operate legally.

Markovic's economic reforms met with some initial success, including a decline in the country's inflation rate. His efforts enjoyed a great deal of early support from the people, which resulted in a high level of popularity for Markovic.

The support did not last, however, in part because leaders of the individual republics were leery of any actions that would make the national Yugoslavian government more powerful. Their reasoning was that a more powerful national government might weaken the republics' power base.

With no political backing from the republics, Markovic had little choice but to sit back and watch as his push for economic reform fizzled out. Ultimately, the shock therapy program backfired. In the wake of economic changes, nearly one million Yugoslavian workers either lost their jobs or were forced to work without pay because their employers could not afford the payroll.

Markovic's popularity began to dip as shock therapy's negative consequences spread across Yugoslavia. As Markovic's position

ANTE MARKOVIC, SHOWN HERE IN 1989, WAS THE PRIME MINISTER OF
Yugoslavia's FEC. He supported free-market solutions to economic chaos.

weakened, Slobodan Milosevic saw an opportunity. He used his
post as president of Serbia to convince people that the capitalistic
motives of Markovic and the Western governments were harmful
to Serbia. Worse for Markovic, the Yugoslavian army, hoping to
increase its own power, threw its support behind Milosevic, further
strengthening the Serbian cause.

FOCUS ON KOSOVO

By 1989 Slobodan Milosevic held considerable power in
Yugoslavia. His political connections gave him control over voting

in the FEC and in both the Yugoslavian and Serbian legislatures. He could decide which candidates would be elected to posts that were of interest to him, and no one could gain office without his approval.

With his power secure, Milosevic then turned his attention to Kosovo. He attacked political opponents by claiming that they were ignoring the oppression of Serbs in the province. He used the Serbs' long-held prejudice against Muslims, who made up the majority in Kosovo, to fuel anger against the Albanians.

Yugoslavia's economic collapse added to the anger. By 1989 inflation had reached a rate of over 60 percent per month. Serbs were desperate for someone to blame, and Milosevic offered them a scapegoat—the Albanian Muslims. In the summer of 1989, Milosevic's dedication to the Serbs was further proven. In July he managed to push through a series of changes to the Serbian constitution that made Kosovo far more dependent on Serbia and more subject to Serbia's authority. One key change was that the Serbian government was authorized to dismiss and then replace any of Kosovo's leaders. The replacements would be people who were strong supporters of Serbs.

Not surprisingly, Serbia's move was highly controversial. The Kosovo legislature had long resisted control by Serbia. Lawmakers were so angry that they voted to create the Republic of Kosovo, an independent republic within Yugoslavia that was not part of Serbia.

Milosevic had a keen interest in keeping Kosovo within Serbia, largely because so many Serbs lived in the province. He was unwilling to cast them adrift to fend for themselves under an ethnic Albanian government. As Serbia's president, he felt he had the authority to force Kosovo to bend to his will.

ISLAM IN THE FORMER YUGOSLAVIA

Yugoslavia was home to millions of Muslims. Founded in the Middle East in the A.D. 600s, Islam eventually spread around the world. Many people in the Balkans converted to Islam during the years of Ottoman rule. In Yugoslavia in the twentieth century, about one-third of the population of Bosnia-Herzegovina was Muslim. The population of Kosovo was predominantly Albanian Muslim.

In some places in the Middle East, Islamic leaders impose strict religious laws on society. For example, women must cover their heads, faces, and bodies in public. Drinking alcohol is forbidden. In the Muslim areas of Yugoslavia, however, such rules were often ignored or modified. For instance, few Muslim women in Yugoslavia covered their entire bodies in public. Bars were both legal and popular, even though Islamic law forbids the drinking of alcohol. In many ways, the Christians and Muslims of Yugoslavia lived very similar lives, not all that different from the way people lived in Europe and the United States.

When the Kosovo legislature voted for the province's change in status, Milosevic's government in Belgrade responded by dissolving the Kosovo legislature. In turn, the large Albanian population in Kosovo rioted, leading to dozens of deaths and thousands of arrests of ethnic Albanians.

Many of Kosovo's Albanians then took their demands for independence underground. They began to meet secretly in homes and in many ways withdrew from public life. They provided education and health care to their own people and sought money from ethnic Albanians living outside the republic to avoid being financially dependent on Serbia.

POLICE OFFICERS CLUB AN ETHNIC ALBANIAN PROTESTER IN KOSOVO in March 1989. Police used tear gas and a water cannon to try to disperse the crowds.

CHAPTER 5

BREAKUP

WHEN SLOBODAN MILOSEVIC BLOCKED KOSOVO'S MOVE toward independence from the rest of Serbia, people in other Yugoslavian republics grew alarmed. People throughout Yugoslavia suspected that Milosevic might pursue a unitary, Serbian-based government for all of Yugoslavia—that is, one central government with authority over the entire country. They thought he would try to increase his control, just as he had done in Kosovo. They feared he would weaken the republics and consolidate the national government's power.

Slovenia was the first republic to take action to protect itself. On September 27, 1989, Slovenia's legislature added fifty-four amendments to the republic's constitution. One of these amendments gave Slovenia the right to secede (declare independence) from the rest of Yugoslavia.

Milosevic was not pleased with Slovenia's actions. For one thing,

MILOSEVIC VOTES ON PARTY amendments at the third day of Communist Party meetings on January 22, 1990.

each republic was supposed to consult with the others before making major constitutional changes such as those that Slovenia had approved in September (although Serbia had not sought approval from the other republics in blocking Kosovo's move toward independence).

In response to what Slovenia had done, Milosevic called a meeting of the nation's Communist Party leaders on

January 20, 1990. The meeting was called the Fourteenth Congress of the League of Communists of Yugoslavia. Milosevic's plan for the meeting was to force the Slovenian delegates to back down from their talk of separation from the rest of the federation. He tried to accomplish this by making sure that Slovenia's representatives were not given an opportunity to gain support from the other republics during the meeting. Milosevic's supporters voted down all the proposals that the Slovenian delegates put forward, and Milosevic said the group representing Slovenia was too small to be of any importance. The Slovenians soon decided that their continued presence at the meeting was useless, and they left. In an unexpected show of support, Croatia's leaders went with them.

Bosnia-Herzegovina's and Macedonia's leaders refused to conduct business at the meeting without Slovenia and Croatia present. The meeting ended with nothing resolved, except that the LCY had officially broken up. Pressure and bickering within Yugoslavia had caused the country's one legal political party to dissolve during its Fourteenth Congress. After that, new political parties emerged within the individual republics, but there was no longer a unified national party.

STRONGMAN

As discontent within the republics grew, Milosevic tightened his grip on power in Serbia. He wanted it to appear that he supported the popular anti-Communist changes that were sweeping Eastern Europe at the time, even though he himself was a solid Communist. To that end, he changed the name of Serbia's League of Communists to the Socialist Party of Serbia. This move helped increase his support within Serbia, as did his continued talk about Serb nationalism.

He also managed to force through some amendments to the republic's constitution. One of these constitutional changes put control of Serbia's armed forces in the hands of its president—Slobodan Milosevic.

Milosevic had a tight grip on his own republic of Serbia, but he knew that Slovenia and Croatia were building up their own military power. At elections held in 1990, the two republics chose presidents and legislators who supported democracy. These new leaders feared Milosevic and sought to protect their own republics from Serbian control. To boost their defenses, they began purchasing weapons on the international market.

Milosevic wanted to build up his own military power in response, so he created the Serbian Volunteer Guard. This was a paramilitary group—that is, a force of civilians who perform some military activities. Its leader was Zeljko Raznjatovic, commonly known as Arkan. Arkan had a long history of working for the Yugoslavian government. During the

MILOSEVIC PUT ZELJKO RAZNJATOVIC (known as Arkan) in charge of the Serbian Volunteer Guard.

1970s, he had operated as an agent throughout Europe. One of his duties was to assassinate Yugoslavian citizens living in Europe who had spoken out against Tito's government. Because of this history, Milosevic's handpicked leader was not popular.

LETTING GO

In addition to Slovenia, Macedonia and Croatia also began to consider declaring independence from the rest of Yugoslavia. Croatia was home to a small number of Serbs, who were unhappy with their republic's plans to pull out of Yugoslavia, so in 1990, they declared pockets of land within the republic to be independent of the Croatian government. They called these areas the Republic of Serbian Krajina.

Milosevic was president of only Serbia, so technically it was not his job to hold Yugoslavia together. However, Serbia was the largest of the republics, so it held a considerable amount of power over the other five. And Milosevic had the allegiance of government officials at both the republic and national levels, whose job *was* to protect Yugoslavia as a whole. As Yugoslavia began to break apart, Milosevic was able to openly exert his power. He sent money and soldiers to different regions of Yugoslavia and pulled strings behind the scenes to keep his supporters in power.

Croatia and Slovenia were the first of the six republics to vote for independence. Both scheduled the launch of their independent nations for June 25, 1991. As the day approached, the Yugoslavian People's Army (YPA) prepared to stop the secession plans by positioning its troops along Slovenia's southern border. On June 27,

YPA soldiers clashed with Slovenians along the border and in the Slovenian capital, Ljubljana. Ten days later, after about fifty people had been killed, the European Union (EU)—an economic and political association of European states—negotiated a cease-fire between the enemy fighters.

Western leaders had supported Yugoslavia since the mid-twentieth century. They hoped it would remain a unified nation and not crumble into civil war. But they also recognized that the only way to keep Slovenia in Yugoslavia was through military force, and they decided it was not worth the effort.

Milosevic, for his part, was willing to accept Slovenian independence because Slovenia had a very small Serb population. One advantage of letting Slovenia go was that it left the YPA available to fight in Croatia. After a three-month waiting period required under the terms of the cease-fire, Slovenia became an independent nation.

Croatia's struggle for independence was much longer and harder than Slovenia's. Croatia was Yugoslavia's second most populous republic, with approximately 4.5 million residents. It was home to a substantial number of Serbs, who wanted to remain in Yugoslavia and had already declared independence from Croatia in 1990.

To keep the Croats from seceding, the Yugoslavian government sent in YPA troops. The Croatian Serbs, who opposed secession, fought alongside the YPA. Milosevic, in support of his fellow Serbs, also backed the effort to keep Croatia from seceding. As with Slovenia, Milosevic had no legal right to intervene in Croatia, because he led Serbia, not Yugoslavia as a whole. All the same, he supplied the Croatian Serbs with money and fighters from his own republic.

Under Milosevic's influence, the YPA engaged in a long, bloody war with Croatia to keep it in the federation. In the course of the fighting, Croatian cities suffered heavy damage, and Serbs took over parts of Croatia. By this time, the chaos in Yugoslavia had gained international attention. To end the destruction and bloodshed, the United Nations sent soldiers to Croatia. They managed to bring an end to the violence. Croatia established its independence, although Serbia did not formally recognize it.

A YUGOSLAV ARMY SOLDIER SURVEYS THE BODIES OF CROATIAN GUARDS killed during fighting for Croatian independence in November 1991.

TWO MORE

The next Yugoslavian republic to declare its independence was Macedonia, on September 8, 1991. Macedonia's exit from Yugoslavia was the most peaceful. The republic had a very small number of Serbs living within its borders, which meant that Milosevic and Serbia had little interest in keeping a hold on it. The Yugoslavian government removed its YPA troops from Macedonia, and it became independent.

Bosnia-Herzegovina was the next battleground for independence. Serbs made up approximately 35 percent of Bosnia-Herzegovina's population at that time, so they were a significant force in the republic. The rest of the republic was primarily made up of Croats and Bosnian Muslims (the largest group; also known as Bosniaks). In November 1991, the Bosnian Serbs voted to create an independent Serb state within Bosnia. They wanted this state to be part of Serbia and Montenegro.

The government of Bosnia-Herzegovina did not recognize the Bosnian Serbs' vote for independence. Instead, the rest of the republic's population took a vote in the spring of 1992. They overwhelmingly chose independence from Yugoslavia. Bosnia's Serbs had boycotted the election, so their voices were not included in the results.

On April 5, 1992, Bosnia-Herzegovina officially declared independence from Yugoslavia. But both Milosevic in Serbia and the Yugoslavian government refused to let Bosnia go. There were too many Serbs in the republic, and those Serbs were demanding independence of their own. The stage was set for a civil war between the Bosnian Serbs and the rest of the nation.

THE BOSNIAN WAR

War erupted within Bosnia-Herzegovina, with Bosnian Serbs fighting against Bosnian Croats and Bosniaks. Milosevic, meanwhile, supported Serb control over a large region of Bosnia-Herzegovina, and he was willing to commit troops from Serbia to fight for it.

As the fighting heated up, Bosnia-Herzegovina's Serbs moved forward with plans for an independent republic of their own. With the help of Serbian troops, they began the process of ridding selected regions of their republic of non-Serb inhabitants, specifically Bosnian Muslims. This program, which came to be called ethnic cleansing, included mass murder, torture, imprisonment, and rape. Bosnian Serb fighters removed vast numbers of Bosnia-Herzegovina's Muslim people by either ejecting them from the republic or slaughtering them outright. The soldiers and commanders on the ground were directly responsible for these acts, but they worked under the authority of and with the approval of Slobodan Milosevic in Belgrade.

When these atrocities began, people around the world took notice. Film crews showed footage of thousands of refugees displaced from their homes. Witnesses and victims told stories of murders and rapes. People around the world began to demand that their governments step in to stop the violence in Bosnia-Herzegovina. Meanwhile, the Serbs managed to seize control of 70 percent of Bosnia's land during the war, while Bosnia-Herzegovina's Croat fighters claimed a large amount of territory for themselves.

The international community imposed sanctions (formal punishments) against Serbia, including a trade embargo (cutting off international trade). The intent was to put economic pressure on Serbia so

A MEMBER OF THE SERBIAN VOLUNTEER GUARD KICKS BODIES OF BOSNIAN
Muslims in March 1992. The paramilitary unit, often called Arkan's Tigers, was responsible for killing thousands of people during the Bosnian War.

that it would stop the fighting and ethnic cleansing. The trade embargo did not end the violence in Bosnia. It did, however, have devastating effects on the Serbian economy, including food shortages, hyperinflation, and unemployment rates topping 50 percent in 1993.

With inflation running wild and other serious economic problems, Milosevic finally agreed to go along with a UN proposal for Bosnian peace. In the spring of 1993, the United Nations presented a peace treaty called the Vance-Owen Plan to the Bosnian Serbs, who by then had set up their own government in the remote Bosnian mountain city of Pale. Milosevic supported the plan, but the Bosnian Serbs, led by Biljana Plavsic and Momcilo Krajisnik, rejected it.

With the rejection of the Vance-Owen Plan, Milosevic lost a great deal of prestige in the eyes of the international community. He had once been viewed around the world as a man who could speak for the entire Serb population of Yugoslavia. His inability to maintain this authority reduced his usefulness to other world leaders.

BLOOD AND MONEY

The trade embargo and the war had taken their toll on the Serbian economy. To finance its military efforts, the Serbian government kept printing money until it was essentially worthless. Inflation reached an all-time high of more than 1,000,000 percent in early 1994, with more than half the population out of work, store shelves empty, and international trade at a standstill because of the embargo.

In an effort to turn things around, Milosevic put Dragoslav Avramovic in charge of the Yugoslavian National Bank. Avramovic's approach was much like Ante Markovic's shock therapy had been several years earlier. He allowed no more money to be printed, and he supported some free-market economic changes. Within months, the inflation rate was down to manageable levels.

But the economy did not fully recover. Throughout Serbia, crime and bribery had become the norm. People bought goods on the black market—an illegal network of buying and selling. To make matters worse, Serbia was playing host to hundreds of thousands of mostly Serb refugees from Bosnia and other war-torn places. Serbia could not afford to feed or house them, let alone provide them with jobs. Even many citizens who were lucky enough to have jobs protested the economy's poor conditions. Life in Serbia was bleak.

RADOVAN KARADZIC

Radovan Karadzic was a key figure in the Bosnian War. A Serb, he was born in Montenegro in 1945. Trained as a psychiatrist, he worked at a Sarajevo hospital, where he got into trouble for selling fake psychiatric reports that would allow people to retire early or to plead insanity when accused of crimes.

In the late 1980s, Karadzic joined the fight for Serb nationalism. He founded the Serbian Democratic Party, which sought to organize Serbs in Bosnia and Croatia in an effort to keep those two republics from declaring independence from the rest of Yugoslavia. When Bosnia-Herzegovina declared its independence on March 1, 1990, Karadzic declared an independent republic of Serbs on Bosnian territory. This republic would come to be called Republika Srpska, and Karadzic was elected its president.

The International Criminal Tribunal for the former Yugoslavia (ICTY, the same body that tried Milosevic) charges that Karadzic committed a variety of war crimes during the Bosnian War. As leader of the Bosnian Serbs, he allegedly ordered the massacre of thousands of non-Serb Bosnians (including the men at Srebrenica), drove thousands more from their homes, and had others locked up in concentration camps.

After the war in Bosnia ended, the ICTY was unable to find Karadzic to bring him to trial. On July 18, 2008, authorities finally arrested him in Belgrade, where he had been posing openly for years as an expert on natural healing. He had grown a bushy beard and long hair to disguise himself and used two false names to hide his true identity.

In 2009 Karadzic appeared before a judge at The Hague. He was charged with eleven counts of war crimes. Karadzic argued that the ICTY had no right to try him. He refused to plead guilty or not guilty to the charges, so the judge entered not-guilty pleas on his behalf. His trial will begin sometime later in 2009.

SERBIAN POLICE GUARD A GROUP OF BOSNIAN MUSLIM MEN FROM Srebrenica, Bosnia-Herzegovina, in August 1995. Serb forces later massacred most of the men.

The fighting continued in Bosnia, putting even the reputation of the United Nations at stake. It sent in peacekeeping troops yet could not manage to make a dent in the violence. The slaughter reached its peak in July 1995 when Bosnian Serb soldiers attacked the town of Srebrenica in Bosnia-Herzegovina. Tens of thousands of Bosnian Muslims had taken refuge in the town, which had been designated a UN safe area—a place where civilians were supposed to be safe from attack. The Serb fighters ignored this designation and advanced on the town. A small force of Dutch UN peacekeeping troops failed to protect the refugees. Over the course of several weeks, Serb fighters rounded up more than eight thousand unarmed Muslim men and boys. The Serbs forced some of the men to dig their own graves before being shot. They hunted down others who tried to flee to the forests outside the town. The massacre shocked the world and led to increased cries for international intervention.

After the Srebrenica attack, anti-Serb forces began strengthening. Part of the increased strength came from large numbers of Bosnian Croat and Muslim refugees who became fighters. In addition, Croatia's army took up arms against the Serbs, and in late 1995, air forces of the North Atlantic Treaty Organization (NATO) joined the alliance against the Serbs. (NATO is an international organization formed to provide military protection to member nations. Member countries are primarily European but also include the United States and Canada.) This large influx of troops offered the Bosnian Croats and Muslims a chance they were eager to take. They began to gain ground in the fight.

Finally, on October 12, 1995, the warring parties called a

U.S. MARINES ARRIVE IN Bosnia-Herzegovina in 1995. Many Western nations, including the United States, joined in the NATO-led fight against the Serbs and later helped enforce peace in Bosnia.

cease-fire throughout Bosnia-Herzegovina. The next month, the United States negotiated an agreement called the Dayton Accord, which finally succeeded in ending the Bosnia-Herzegovina War. The treaty required that Serbia recognize the independence of Bosnia-Herzegovina and Croatia. When the treaty was signed, the international community lifted economic sanctions against Serbia.

THE DAYTON PEACE TALKS

Achieving peace in Bosnia—although it looked like an impossible task—was a high priority for U.S. president Bill Clinton. People in the United States and Europe were appalled to see the horrors of ethnic cleansing in Srebrenica and elsewhere on the nightly news. Europe had experienced similar horrors during World War II, when Adolf Hitler's government had imprisoned and killed six million European Jews, as well as millions of other minority peoples.

Determined to stop the carnage, President Clinton hosted talks between the opposing forces to bring about a peace treaty. Talks took place at Wright-Patterson Air Force Base, just outside Dayton, Ohio, beginning on November 1, 1995. Slobodan Milosevic attended the talks along with three Bosnian Serb delegates. The Bosnian Croats and Bosniaks also sent representatives. Because of the conference's location, the resulting treaty was known as the Dayton Accord.

MILOSEVIC *(SECOND FROM LEFT, FRONT ROW)* **SIGNS THE DAYTON ACCORD,** along with other Yugoslavian leaders, in December 1995. U.S. president Bill Clinton *(second from left, back row)* helped negotiate the treaty for peace in Bosnia.

During the conference, controversy centered on which ethnic groups would control which parts of Bosnia. The proposed map of Bosnia changed many times during the peace talks. The whole time, Milosevic behaved like a smooth politician interested in negotiating peace. He even made the final gesture that enabled the parties to reach agreement, letting the Bosnian Muslims take control of the republic's capital city of Sarajevo.

The loss of Sarajevo was a disappointment to the Bosnian Serbs, who had desperately wanted the city as their own. In fact, the Bosnian Serb delegates did not want to sign the agreement. Milosevic stepped in and promised his U.S. hosts that he would take care of that problem. He said, "I guarantee you that I will have their signatures within twenty-two hours of my return to Belgrade." Milosevic still wielded enough power to make good on his promise. He saw to it that the delegates signed the Dayton Accord, and the war was ended.

CHAPTER 6

A NEW

WHEN SLOVENIA, CROATIA, MACEDONIA, AND BOSNIA-HERZEGOVINA

abandoned Yugoslavia, the remaining republics of Serbia and
Montenegro established a new government. They called themselves the Federal Republic of Yugoslavia (FRY) and wrote a new
constitution.

The FRY was supposed to be a republic, a government that
derives its power from the people—a bottom-up approach in
which power flows from those who are governed up to their
elected leaders, who have responsibility for administering the
government on behalf of the people. Despite this label, Slobodan
Milosevic and his colleagues held the reins of government firmly
in the new Yugoslavia, and the common people had relatively little
control over their country.

In theory, the new constitution established equality between

the republics of Serbia and Montenegro. The legislature—the
120-member National Chamber of Citizens—contained the same
number of members from both Montenegro and Serbia. Each
republic elected its own president, and the national legislature
chose a president for the nation as a whole (called a federal president). The legislature also selected a prime minister, and it was
generally accepted that he or she would come from Serbia if the
federal president was from Montenegro and from Montenegro if the
federal president was from Serbia.

Despite these checks designed to guarantee the equality of
Serbia and Montenegro, everyone knew that Serbia was the dominant force in the nation. Slobodan Milosevic remained the president
of Serbia and used his personal power and connections to maintain
a tight hold on government.

The FRY constitution provided for a variety of personal freedoms to the people of the new Yugoslavia. For instance, all political parties, both Communist and non-Communist, were legal under the new constitution. People were allowed to assemble and protest freely, and freedom of the press was guaranteed. The authorities were not allowed to search people's homes without warrants (authorizations by judges or other officials).

Milosevic and his government commonly ignored these freedoms, however. For instance, the government regularly squashed the right to free speech, including a free press. It controlled most of the media and made sure that non-Communist political parties had no access to government-run media outlets.

AN UNPOPULAR PRESIDENT

By 1996 Slobodan Milosevic's popularity and tight control over Serbia were both in a downward spiral. A number of local elections were held that year, and the results demonstrated just how unpopular his repressive government had become. In many of the elections, voters chose candidates who opposed Milosevic and his government. Milosevic immediately responded by invalidating the results of the elections.

Throughout Serbia, citizens were outraged. Their legally elected opposition candidates could not take office. However, the Serbian people had few choices available to them for voicing their anger. They knew that any antigovernment violence would surely be met with violence from Milosevic's army. Also, Milosevic tightly controlled the media. Large newspapers and television were in government hands, leaving few ways for citizens to express themselves.

Despite the restrictions placed upon them by Milosevic, the Serbian people soon struck upon a new way to respond to unpopular government action: peaceful protest. In particular, they began to publicly ignore official, government-censored TV news programs. Instead of sitting inside watching TV, they would either go outdoors or make so much noise inside that it was impossible to hear the broadcasts. People began wearing whistles and blowing them in protest of the untruths that the government spread through the media.

Milosevic's government tried to stop the protests, but the sheer number of them made it impossible. Milosevic finally compromised by allowing some legally elected opposition candidates to take their seats in local government. He would not, however, allow them access to the local media outlets. At one point, Belgrade police officers locked themselves in radio and television studios to keep elected opposition leaders out.

PRESIDENT OF YUGOSLAVIA

In 1996 Milosevic was finishing his second four-year term as Serbia's president. According to the FRY constitution, two terms was the limit, so Milosevic needed another influential government position to remain in power in Yugoslavia. The job of president of the Federal Republic of Yugoslavia suited his goals perfectly.

By this time, his popularity was low—but it was the legislature, not the voters, who would choose the FRY president in July 1997.

Milosevic's wife, Mirjana, was a powerful force in this election. During the November 1996 legislative elections, she had led a powerful political party called Yugoslav United Left, which helped elect pro-Communist candidates. During the presidential elections in July, those winning candidates were in a position to select Milosevic for president.

The election was not without its troubles for Milosevic and his supporters, however. The plan had been for Milosevic to take the job being vacated by his political ally Zoran Lilic, while Lilic ran for Milosevic's old seat as president of Serbia. However, under the Serbian constitution, the successful candidate had to win more than 50 percent of the votes, and Lilic did not get sufficient votes to win. It took three rounds of voting for a candidate to emerge with enough votes, and it wasn't Lilic but a man named Milan Milutinovic. Without Lilic on board as president of Serbia, Milosevic lost a great deal of power in his republic.

MILOSEVIC AND HIS WIFE, Mirjana, arrive at a polling station to vote in the November 1996 legislative elections.

THE PEOPLE SURROUNDING MILOSEVIC

Slobodan Milosevic surrounded himself with people whom he could control. Some of them were single-minded in their nationalist loyalty, while others were simply violent thugs. He expected his associates to be fiercely loyal and do exactly what he ordered them to do without question. Milosevic had a distrustful nature, and he avoided having the same people around him for very long. When someone had finished a job, he did not hesitate to replace that person with someone new.

He did not share his plans and ambitions with others, preferring to keep them secret—a tactic he had learned early on as a young member of the Communist Party. At that time, he had learned that those who expressed an interest in power tended to see their political careers end quickly.

With his habits of expecting unquestioning loyalty and not confiding in anyone, Milosevic did not have many trusted colleagues. "Milosevic knows only servants and enemies," his former information minister Aleksandar Tijanic said. "Partners and allies do not exist for him."

NEXT BATTLEGROUND: KOSOVO

Even though most of the republics had already seceded, peace was still not on the horizon for what was left of Yugoslavia. The dispute between Serbia and Kosovo over Kosovo's independence had been brewing for many years. Kosovo's majority population of Albanian

Muslims disliked the growing power of the FRY government under Slobodan Milosevic.

As the FRY's new president, Milosevic had control over the YPA, which by 1997 was primarily made up of Serbs. Milosevic used the YPA as well as Serbian troops to fight Albanian rebels in Kosovo. The rebel force, called the Kosovo Liberation Army (KLA), was an unofficial military force, since Kosovo was not an independent country and had no legal right to create its own army.

The KLA attacked troops from both Serbia and the FRY, as well as any individuals who opposed Kosovo's independence movement. Milosevic publically described KLA members as terrorists who used tactics such as torture and the murder of civilians as part of their battle strategy. He argued that he had no choice but to fight them.

Battles between the KLA and YPA continued until 1999, when full-scale war broke out. To escape the violence, thousands of Albanian Muslims fled Kosovo and streamed into neighboring countries. Once again, charges of ethnic cleansing emerged from the war-torn region. Once again, Slobodan Milosevic was seen as the mastermind behind the atrocities. Observers accused Milosevic's forces of herding Albanians not just out of Kosovo but completely out of Serbia into bordering nations, including Albania and Macedonia.

REFUGEES FROM KOSOVO MAKE their way down a mountain into Albania in 1998. Thousands of Albanian Muslims fled Kosovo during the YPA-KLA conflict.

KOSOVO LIBERATION ARMY

In 2007, many years after the Kosovo War ended, an article in the *New Yorker* magazine shed light on how members of the KLA *(such as those shown below running into battle in 1998)* experienced the war. By then Kosovo's prime minister was a man named Agim Ceku, who had served as a KLA general in the war with Serbia. During the conflict, Serbian soldiers had killed Ceku's father and forty other men in his village.

Ceku said that the Kosovars had not merely been fighting for an independent state but had fought for the very survival of the Albanian Muslims in Kosovo. The article explained that Milosevic's troops drove almost one million Albanian Muslims from the province. They took refuge in Macedonia, Montenegro, and Albania.

The article went on to quote Agim Ceku as saying, "The Serbian intention was to end the war without any KLA left. . . . We lost a lot of soldiers." Indeed, the KLA lost at least fifteen thousand of its approximately thirty-five thousand fighters during the war.

YPA soldiers allegedly raped Albanian women, often in their own homes and with their families present. For their part, the KLA allegedly kidnapped and murdered civilians who supported the Serb cause.

The fighting between the YPA and the KLA was brutal. One particularly horrific example was the Racak Massacre, near the village of Racak, Kosovo, a hotbed of KLA activity. First, KLA forces killed four Serb police officers there. In retaliation, YPA forces killed forty to forty-five ethnic Albanians. Several women and an adolescent boy were among the dead, and some victims had been decapitated. In its defense, the YPA charged that every person killed in Racak had been a member of the KLA and had died fighting YPA forces.

As images of slaughter flew around the globe, outrage mounted. Once again, people called for international intervention to halt the bloodshed and ethnic cleansing. On March 24, 1999, NATO

AN ETHNIC ALBANIAN MAN LOOKS DOWN ON THE BODIES OF FORTY massacred ethnic Albanians. Found on a hillside in the village of Racak, Kosovo, in 1999, some of the bodies had been mutilated.

NATO FIGHTERS IN SERBIAN SKIES

NATO fighter pilots who dropped multiton bombs on Serbian targets worked amid danger and fear. Serbian forces fought them with surface-to-air missiles and fighter jets. The fighter pilots had to use evasive maneuvers to escape enemy attacks.

While the NATO pilots risked their lives, they also made some tragic mistakes. Sometimes NATO bombs missed their military targets and killed civilians instead. On May 24, 1999, *US News and World Report* wrote, "Mistakes made by various NATO aircraft have cost the lives of dozens of Serbian civilians and Kosovar refugees. Last week, Yugoslavian authorities accused NATO of killing 79 more refugees with errant [off-target] bombs near the town of Prizren [in Kosovo]."

In the end, NATO's bombs caused tremendous destruction in Serbia. Damage to roads, utilities, and public buildings was estimated at $4 billion. Reconstruction continues into the twenty-first century, although funding is scarce and many projects have been put on hold.

planes began to bomb Serbian targets in an attempt to force Milosevic to withdraw his troops. The bombing campaign reduced huge sections of Serbia and Kosovo to rubble and destroyed an estimated one-third of Yugoslavia's military power. Serbia's water, telephone, and electrical services were also badly damaged, causing great suffering throughout the republic. After seventy-eight days, Milosevic signed on to the Kumanovo Agreement. In this treaty, he agreed to pull out of Kosovo, and NATO stopped its bombing campaign.

By pulling his troops out of Kosovo, Milosevic left an absence of government control in the province. As a result, the United Nations was in the position of keeping the peace and governing the province. Among other tensions, the UN faced Albanian Muslim anger about their treatment at the hands of the YPA. The United Nations worried that Albanians might take out this anger on the Serbs. For their part, the Serbs did not believe the UN peacekeepers could keep them safe. Therefore, many of them fled Kosovo.

END OF A PRESIDENCY

By this time, Yugoslavia was a shadow of the country it had been when Slobodan Milosevic became Serbia's president. What remained was teetering on the brink of collapse. Yet Milosevic was reluctant to give up his hold on power. By then the United Nations had created the International Criminal Tribunal for the former Yugoslavia to try cases of war crimes arising from the country's civil wars.

On May 27, 1999, the tribunal charged Milosevic with war crimes for his actions during the Kosovo War. He refused to give himself up to the UN tribunal, however, and remained in his position as Yugoslavia's president. The ICTY had no authority to invade Yugoslavia to arrest Milosevic.

By 2000 Milosevic had only one year left in his four-year term as Yugoslavia's president. He wished to remain president, but the FRY constitution limited each president to only one term. The only way for Milosevic to legally stay in office was to amend the constitution.

As usual, Serbian representatives controlled the Yugoslavian legislature, and Milosevic controlled many of them. He used his

MILOSEVIC WAVES TO SUPPORTERS in 1999. The United Nations charged him with war crimes that same year.

influence to pass several key changes to the constitution. One amendment changed the president's maximum number of four-year terms from one to three. Milosevic also changed the nation's election process. Previously, the legislature had selected the president, but Milosevic had the system changed so the people could vote directly.

He was certain the people would vote for him in a new presidential election. While he was not enjoying high popularity, his opponents were not well organized. Also, many Yugoslavians were angrier at the international community for economic sanctions and bombings than they were at Milosevic. They might not have liked their president, but they believed that keeping him in office would be a slap in the face to what many saw as the country's international oppressors.

Milosevic's term would not expire until July 2001. Nevertheless, he felt confident in his success and called for an early election to take place on September 24, 2000. When the results came in, they showed that Milosevic had taken second place behind opposition candidate

Vojislav Kostunica. What's more, an alliance of political parties called the Democratic Opposition of Serbia, led by Zoran Djindic, had won a large majority of seats in the Yugoslavian legislature. It was a final decisive defeat for Slobodan Milosevic and his Communist colleagues. Yet even in the face of this clear defeat, Milosevic refused to accept the election results nor would he participate in the runoff election required by the FRY constitution whenever no candidate received 50 percent or more of the vote.

The Yugoslavian people were furious that Milosevic would not accept the election results, and they began to protest. Milosevic's grip on power loosened quickly in the face of this opposition. The army and paramilitary forces led by Arkan did not support him enough to stop the demonstrations, and opposition forces took over

HUNDREDS OF THOUSANDS OF PROTESTERS GATHER IN FRONT OF THE federal parliament building in Belgrade to demand Milosevic's resignation.

a key television station. Finally, on October 5, 2000, a massive crowd gathered outside the legislature and demanded that Milosevic give up his seat as president.

Milosevic met with Vojislav Kostunica the next day, and on October 7, 2000, Yugoslavia had a new president. For the first time in many years, Slobodan Milosevic was not part of the government in Yugoslavia.

LIFE IN YUGOSLAVIA while Slobodan Milosevic held power was a tragic mix of relative comfort and unspeakable brutality. During Milosevic's early political career, many Yugoslavians enjoyed a relatively high standard of living. However, the wars that broke out in Croatia, Bosnia, and Kosovo were a horrifying reminder that peace was in scarce supply in Yugoslavia. And Milosevic's methods of maintaining control over his people denied them many basic rights.

WOMEN AND CHILDREN

Life in Milosevic's Yugoslavia was largely focused on the family. Both in cities and rural areas, family relationships were of tremen-

YUGOSLAVIA

PEOPLE IN SLOVENIA GATHER AT AN OUTDOOR MARKET. COMPARED TO residents of other Communist countries, people in Yugoslavia enjoyed a fairly high standard of living in the late twentieth century.

dous importance. Rural farming families needed many hands to work the land, so it was common for extended families (including grandparents, aunts, uncles, and cousins) to live together. In urban areas, people still felt a strong connection to family, although extended families did not commonly live together in cities.

Birthrates in Yugoslavia varied greatly, depending on the republic or province. Kosovo's birthrate was higher than that of any other region in Yugoslavia (and the highest in all Europe), partly because women married young, typically around the age of eighteen, and didn't complete much schooling. Rather than taking jobs outside the home, they tended to be homemakers and have many children. The province's population soared by 220 percent between 1950 and 1983, while the population of Yugoslavia as a whole climbed by only 39 percent.

Traditionally, Yugoslavian women did not work outside the home. Over the years of Communist rule, however, more Yugoslavian women took jobs. By 1987 women made up 38 percent of the labor force in nonfarming jobs. But again, the numbers varied by region. Women were almost half of the workforce in Slovenia, while in Kosovo only 20 percent of workers were female. In that province, a woman's traditional role as wife and mother was more dominant.

YUGOSLAVIAN SCHOOLCHILDREN AND THEIR TEACHER IN THE MID-1990S.
Teaching young children was a traditionally female occupation in Yugoslavia.

Women who did work outside the home held jobs in a variety of areas, including government service and food service. Nearly all the teachers in Yugoslavia's elementary schools were female. Whether or not they had jobs, women in Yugoslavia still bore primary responsibility for cooking and maintaining their homes. The government gave mothers several months paid time off from work after the birth of a child.

Traditionally, men in Yugoslavia were dominant in business and government. But women attempted to improve their status in the late twentieth century. Despite heavy government censorship, female writers created feminist literature. Some women in Belgrade joined an organization called Women in Black to demonstrate against the wars in Bosnia, Slovenia, and Kosovo.

LIFE IN WARTIME

During Yugoslavia's many wars in the 1990s, the quality of life for men, women, and children declined sharply. Warfare and trade embargoes damaged the economy, and everyone suffered as a result of high unemployment and high inflation. But beyond the economic problems, mere survival became challenging for many citizens. For instance, all men between the ages of eighteen and fifty-five were eligible to be drafted into the YPA. One writer claimed that during the Kosovo War, men in Belgrade were reluctant to go out in the streets, because they could be drafted into the military on the spot.

Life in wartime was particularly harsh for women and children. Thousands of children fled with their families to escape invading

THIS REFUGEE CAMP IN ALBANIA, SHOWN IN 1999, HOUSED MANY PEOPLE
who fled Yugoslavia during the wars in the 1990s. The refugees lived in big tents.

armies. In Croatia, Kosovo, and Bosnia, invading armies frequently slaughtered civilians, including children. Soldiers also frequently raped women during the wars.

Many refugee families lived in crowded, dirty camps, spread throughout the former Yugoslavian republics, as well as in neighboring countries. The camps lacked basic services such as electricity and running water. People slept in tents. Instead of indoor flush toilets, they used outdoor pit latrines.

During the Kosovo War, Blace Camp in Macedonia was in particularly poor condition, with trash strewn across the ground and shabby tents erected haphazardly. The camp was home to more than twenty-five thousand Kosovo refugees. Eventually, because of the unhealthy living conditions, Macedonian authorities decided to move the refugees to other camps. But the evacuation was mishandled. Macedonian officials did not allow residents to prepare for the move, and some families ended up split apart into separate camps.

HEALTH CARE

Under Communism, Yugoslavia had a national health-care system, with free medical care provided by the government. The quality of health care varied by region, however. For instance, people in urban areas enjoyed more health-care options and more modern medical facilities than those in rural areas. In special cases, mostly for children, the government sent people abroad for state-of-the-art medical procedures that were not available in Yugoslavia.

In 1982, prior to the Yugoslavian wars, the life expectancy for Yugoslavian men was 67.8 years, while women on average lived to 73.5 years. Many Yugoslavians smoked cigarettes, which led to high cancer rates. The nation's AIDS rate was low. Suicide in the former Yugoslavia cost many lives, including both of Milosevic's parents. The suicide rates, especially high in Croatia and Slovenia, remain a puzzle to researchers.

Social scientists use infant mortality rates to measure the quality of health care in a nation. In 1984 Yugoslavia's infant mortality rate was high, with on average 28.9 infant deaths per 1,000 babies born. This was the second-highest rate in Europe, behind only Albania. The figure varied greatly among Yugoslavia's republics and provinces, however. For instance, Kosovo's infant mortality rate was highest, at 63.1 deaths per 1,000 births. The province of Vojvodina and the republic of Macedonia had the lowest rates, at 12.0 and 15.7 deaths for every 1,000 births, respectively.

Warfare severely strained the national health-care system. Thousands of people died in the country's conflicts, and many thousands more were injured. In Kosovo alone, NATO bombs killed an estimated two thousand civilians and injured another seventy-five hundred. Military casualties were even higher. Caring for the injured was a challenge in the war-torn nation—especially since the fighting damaged many health-care centers. NATO bombings alone destroyed or damaged an estimated thirty-three hospitals and health clinics. After the wars, long-term health concerns remained. Many people lived with permanent injuries, such as lost limbs from bombings and land mines. Soldiers and civilians alike suffered psychological trauma. Many bombed-out hospitals and health clinics were not rebuilt following the wars. Drugs and medical equipment were in short supply. As a result, maternal mortality rates (the number

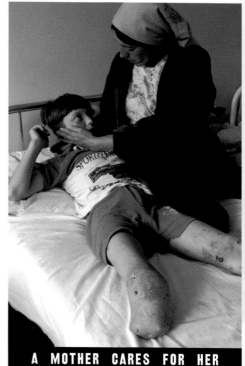

A MOTHER CARES FOR HER twelve-year-old son at a hospital in 1999. The boy lost part of his leg when he stepped on a land mine near his village in Kosovo.

TRAGEDY FOR THE DISABLED

Yugoslavia provided for citizens who could not work due to disability, mental illness, or other impairment. The government ran nursing homes, orphanages, and homes for the disabled who had no family to care for them.

Many of Serbia's homes for the disabled were unclean and inhumane, however. Patients, both old and young, were tied to cribs and beds. The patients were ill, malnourished, and dehydrated. They suffered from weak muscles and deformed bones due to lack of exercise. Overworked staff in the institutions did not have time to cuddle the youngest children, leaving them to grow up with little human contact. Some adults were so malnourished that they were no bigger than children.

A recent study explains that cultural attitudes toward the disabled in Yugoslavia—the desire to hide them away out of sight—were partly to blame. The study reports, "This approach reflects a system which has historically labeled and segregated people identified with a disability, particularly when that disability is intellectual, developmental, or psychiatric in nature."

The situation occurred both during and after the Yugoslavian wars. Some of the homes for the disabled were even brand-new buildings, constructed with money sent from abroad to help the war-torn nation. Despite the new facilities, patients received horrific care there.

of mothers who die from causes related to childbearing) and infant mortality rates rose during and after the wars, and life expectancy dropped.

EDUCATION

Yugoslavia provided public education to all children. The dominant language in classrooms was Serbo-Croatian (sometimes called Croato-Serbian), although the language sometimes varied by region. Children started an eight-year-long primary school education at the age of six or seven. The secondary school (high school) system was specialized, meaning that students chose specialties such as teaching, art, or the military, depending on their future career plans. After three or four years in secondary school, interested and qualified students could go on to college or a university.

LANGUAGE IN YUGOSLAVIA

The people of Yugoslavia spoke a variety of languages, including Serbo-Croatian, Slovenian, Macedonian, Albanian, and Hungarian. The most commonly used language was Serbo-Croatian. This language has three different dialects, or variations, spoken in different regions.

The Serbo-Croatian alphabet has some letters that do not exist in English. For example, the combined letters *dj* are one consonant in Serbo-Croatian, pronounced *d* as in *dune*. Many Serbo-Croatian words are normally written with accent marks, but for ease of reading, the accent marks have been omitted in this book.

As with so many aspects of life in Yugoslavia, the quality and quantity of education varied by location. In 1981 Slovenia had the best educational record, with only 3.6 percent of its adults uneducated and nearly 35 percent of citizens with a high school education. In Kosovo, on the other hand, about 28 percent of adults had no formal education and only 15 percent obtained a high school education. Kosovo's literacy rate (percentage of people who could read and write) was at the bottom too. In 1981 only 82.4 percent of Kosovo's citizens could read, compared to 99.2 percent of Slovenians.

Warfare took a terrible toll on Yugoslavia's educational system. NATO bombs destroyed many schools in Kosovo. Furthermore, child refugees in Yugoslavia had little stability in education because of having to flee their homes. In refugee camps, the chief concern was survival and education was of secondary importance. Despite the difficulties, some groups attempted to provide schooling to displaced children. For instance, the international children's rights organization UNICEF set up schools for Kosovar children in Macedonian refugee camps. In many cases, host families in Macedonia took in refugee families, and children of those families attended local schools.

RELIGION

Communist governments often demand that their citizens abandon religious beliefs and practices. The governments hope that citizens will work together and concentrate on improving their country rather than spending time on religious activities and religious divisions. Yugoslavia followed this pattern after World War II.

Like other Communist leaders, Josip Broz Tito attempted to suppress religious practice among Yugoslavia's citizens. He wanted the nation's diverse ethnic and religious groups to come together as one united country rather than focusing on their differences. For nearly ten years after World War II, the Yugoslavian government jailed, tortured, and executed clergy members of all faiths. As a result of this oppression, the numbers of Yugoslavians who publically expressed religious beliefs declined during Tito's time.

After Tito's death, controls on religion loosened and Yugoslavia experienced an upswing in the number of people who openly practiced their faiths. Slobodan Milosevic and other new leaders did not try to stop this trend. Milosevic was himself an atheist—someone who does not believe in deities—but he claimed in a speech in 1989 that Yugoslavia's religious diversity was part of its strength.

By the late 1980s, Yugoslavians of all faiths felt free to pursue their chosen beliefs. Religion became such a normal part of Yugoslavian life that by 1990, government-run television stations broadcast both Eastern Orthodox and Roman Catholic Easter services. That same year, the Islamic holy month of Ramadan was celebrated with televised prayers.

The people of Yugoslavia had longed for religious expression over many decades, and they embraced freedom of religion during the 1980s and 1990s. However, religious differences that had been buried during Tito's rule bubbled to the surface when people were able to freely practice their beliefs once again.

Most Yugoslavians practiced one of three religions: Eastern Orthodox Christianity, Roman Catholicism, or Islam, although some people practiced other faiths, such as Judaism and Mormonism. Most people practiced the faith of their families and other members of their ethnic group. During Milosevic's rule, 46 percent

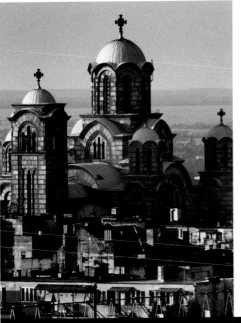

SOME PEOPLE IN YUGOSLAVIA PRACTICED EASTERN ORTHODOX
Christianity. Others were Catholic, while still others were Muslim. The photo at left shows an Orthodox church in Belgrade. The photo on the right shows a Catholic church in Croatia.

of citizens identified themselves as Eastern Orthodox, including almost all the country's Serbs. Another 30 percent of the population was Roman Catholic, including most Croats. Seventeen percent of the population was Muslim, including the large number of ethnic Albanians who lived in Kosovo.

Yugoslavia's religious groups were not clearly divided along republic and provincial borders. The Eastern Orthodox Church was dominant in much of Serbia, Montenegro, and Macedonia. Roman Catholics formed the majority in Croatia and Slovenia. Croatia also was home to many Eastern Orthodox Serbs, while many Catholic Croats made their home in Bosnia-Herzegovina. Muslims were the

ALBANIAN MUSLIMS IN KOSOVO OBSERVE PRAYERS AT THE END OF THE holy month of Ramadan in 2003. During Milosevic's time as president, Muslims enjoyed freedom to practice their faith, but religious differences among the ethnic groups in Yugoslavia later led to war.

clear majority in the province of Kosovo and formed a significant minority in Macedonia, Bosnia-Herzegovina, and Slovenia.

Religious differences played a part in the civil violence and in the calls for independence that marked Yugoslavia under Slobodan Milosevic. For example, the Eastern Orthodox Serbs frequently clashed with Albanian Muslims, and religious intolerance ran high.

ECONOMICS

For many years, Yugoslavia's economy was one of the healthiest in Eastern Europe. Many people could afford luxuries such as cars and vacations. The country was living on money borrowed from other nations, however. When the interest payments on that money grew too large, the prosperity of the country and its people dropped off sharply. As a result, workers began to strike in large numbers, and industrial production dropped. Trade embargoes designed to pressure the republics to stop fighting also took their toll.

Even before Yugoslavia blew up into full-scale civil war, republics began to fight among themselves using economic weapons. Sometimes, after a political argument, one republic would impose trade restrictions on another, cutting off trade in an effort to damage the republic's economy. This pattern was an early sign of rocky relationships to come.

Under Slobodan Milosevic, the Yugoslavian economy was nearly destroyed. He spent extraordinary sums of money on the

IN THE LATE TWENTIETH CENTURY, SOME PEOPLE IN YUGOSLAVIA prospered. In Belgrade (*shown above*) some people had cars and other desirable consumer products.

wars in Croatia, Bosnia, and Kosovo. When the government printed more money, inflation rates soared. During the wars, production in the country's factories and on its farms nearly came to a standstill. Economic sanctions meant that other countries wouldn't buy products produced in Yugoslavia. Sanctions also prevented foreign goods from coming into the country. Making matters worse, Milosevic's government was corrupt, with government officials using public money for their own benefit instead of the people's.

Milosevic's Communist administration attempted to put some government-owned companies into the hands of private investors, a process called privatization. The goal of privatization is to make businesses more efficient by having them operate in the free-market economy. This effort was too little, too late to save the Yugoslavian economy. Workers and government officials alike resisted the efforts. Employees were afraid that the changes would eventually leave them jobless, while government officials did not want to lose their control over the economy. As a result, privatization was largely a failure.

Unemployment rates during Slobodan Milosevic's time in office contributed to the economy's poor performance. In the mid-1990s, more than half of the population was out of work. Although the government was supposed to provide unemployment benefits for those who could not find jobs and welfare benefits for those who were unable to work, those payments were insufficient. In Serbia (excluding Kosovo) only one person in ten who needed welfare benefits bothered to register for them—because people knew that fewer than half of those who did register would receive any money from the government. Some welfare and pension payments were more than a year late. Unemployment benefits were little better, with those payments typically arriving three months late.

ETHNIC GROUPS

In 1990, the year after Milosevic became president of Serbia, Yugoslavia was home to approximately 23.5 million people. The diversity of this population was tremendous. The South Slavs made up more than 80 percent of Yugoslavia's people, and this group was further divided into Serbs, Croats, Muslim Slavs, Slovenes, Macedonians, and Montenegrins. The nation was also home to non–South Slavs, including Albanians, Hungarians, and other minority groups. Following is a breakdown of the populations in Yugoslavia's republics according to the country's 1981 census.

Republic	Population	Primary Ethnic Groups
Bosnia-Herzegovina	4,116,000	Muslim Slavs, Serbs, Croats
Croatia	4,576,000	Croats, Serbs
Macedonia	1,914,000	Macedonians
Montenegro	583,000	Montenegrins
Serbia (excluding Kosovo and Vojvodina)	5,666,000	Serbs
Slovenia	1,884,000	Slovenes

Province		
Kosovo	1,585,000	Albanians, Serbs
Vojvodina	2,028,000	Serbs, Hungarians, Croats

Total Population	22,352,000

Most Yugoslavians identified themselves as members of an ethnic group rather than as Yugoslavs. It was partly ethnic and religious hatreds among these diverse ethnic groups, fueled by nationalistic fever, that led to the Yugoslavian wars.

CHAPTER 8

STRONGMAN

FROM 1946 TO 1990, the Communist Party, officially called the League of Communists of Yugoslavia, was a vitally important part of both government and everyday life in Yugoslavia. During that time, the LCY was the only legal political party in the nation. In addition to the national-level party, each of the republics and provinces had its own unit of the LCY.

By the late 1980s, the LCY had two million members, and all national-, republic-, and provincial-level government officials came from those ranks. The LYC even controlled the nation's judicial system. Judges were named to their positions based on party connections, and the party monitored judges to make sure their rulings were in keeping with party wishes.

The LCY claimed that its goal was to promote Communist ideology in Yugoslavia. However, it was not usually a devotion to

MILOSEVIC *(RIGHT)* **ATTENDS A MEETING OF THE YUGOSLAVIAN COMMUNIST** Party Central Committee in 1988. The Communist Party held power in Yugoslavia for decades.

Communist principles that caused citizens to join the party. They tended to be more practical, joining the party to improve their job prospects. It was well known that the vast majority of the country's politicians, business executives, and military leaders were LCY members. To get ahead, it was wise to join the LCY.

The Socialist Alliance of Working People of Yugoslavia (SAWPY) also played a powerful role in daily life in Yugoslavia. In 1990 this group numbered 13 million members out of a total Yugoslavian population of 23.5 million. The SAWPY worked hand in hand with the LCY to achieve party goals and to create support for Communism. The group's functions, listed in the 1974 Yugoslavian constitution, included overseeing elections and nominating candidates to serve in commune-level political offices.

The National Youth Federation of Yugoslavia was designed to prepare young people for membership in the LCY and SAWPY. In addition, Yugoslavian educators taught Marxist theory in secondary schools and colleges in an attempt to create a population that understood and supported the Communist system.

COMMUNISM LOSES ITS GRIP

Josip Broz Tito had managed to unite the different ethnic groups within the LCY, but after he died in 1980, ethnic tensions began to pull the party in different directions. Membership began to drop and so did the party's influence. When the party broke up in 1990, Yugoslavia entered a new era of political freedom. Multiple political parties became legal and were able to compete with one another for members.

As the party fell apart nationally, Communism also lost its hold in schools and universities. Many students resisted indoctrination in Communist theory. Instead of buying into Communist ideals, they learned about and longed for democracy. Slobodan Milosevic was unhappy to see universities moving away from Communist teaching.

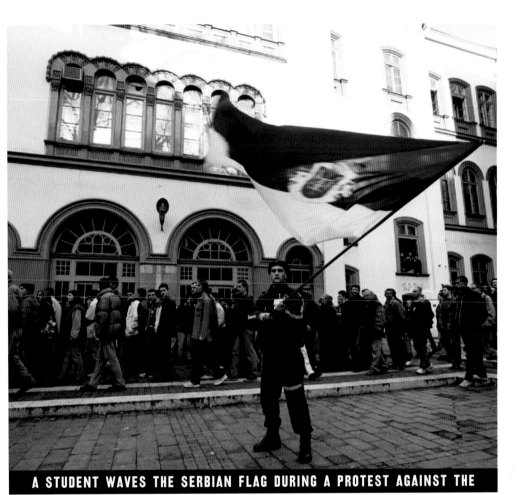

A STUDENT WAVES THE SERBIAN FLAG DURING A PROTEST AGAINST THE
Communist government and Milosevic at the University of Belgrade in 1997.

He and his wife, Mirjana, used their connections in higher education to fight the change, but they could not stop the trend.

Finally, as the country's unemployment rate climbed through the end of the twentieth century, fewer young people were interested in maintaining a Communist-based economy or in joining the LCY. Membership in the National Youth Federation dropped as the country's young people drifted away from Communism.

MEDIA CONTROL

Media censorship had a long history in Yugoslavia, beginning after World War II when Tito took power. After Tito's death, Milosevic and other leaders kept tight control of Yugoslavian media. They used the media to promote Communist ideology and support for the government in general. They also used the media to promote Serb nationalism among different ethnic groups.

The Yugoslavian constitution guaranteed free speech and a free press, but Milosevic's government largely ignored those freedoms. It imposed censorship restrictions on writers and controlled the messages put out by newspapers, magazines, and television stations.

Some newspapers in Yugoslavia were government controlled, while others were independent. But independent papers could not operate without a license from the government, and Milosevic used many tricks to keep them from operating freely. For instance, he sometimes claimed that paper and printing equipment were in short supply and made sure that independent papers couldn't get them. Without this material, independent papers could not get their messages out to citizens. The government-controlled media, meanwhile, turned out a steady stream of support for the president and Serb nationalist propaganda.

Serb author Svetlana Slapsak was one writer who risked speaking out against Milosevic's government. When she wrote about feminism, freedom of expression, and democracy, critics condemned her harshly. In 1987 Slapsak angered the Yugoslavian authorities further when she joined a campaign to free an Albanian political prisoner. The government, including Slobodan Milosevic's wife (then working as a censor) took notice. It pulled Slapsak's regular

FREEDOM OF THE PRESS?

During his reign, Milosevic allowed one weekly news magazine, *Vreme* (Time), to print whatever it wanted without government control, even stories that were not favorable to the government. But letting *Vreme* have some freedom might have been a shrewdly calculated move on Milosevic's part. One scholar suggests that Milosevic allowed *Vreme* to function independently as a way to manipulate people. Milosevic might have tolerated a little bit of press freedom in Yugoslavia to make people think they had more freedom than they really did. The move might have been designed to keep the people moderately happy, so they would not protest or try to overthrow their oppressive government.

column out of a magazine. Government-controlled media then criticized her loudly. The following year, the government had her arrested and tried as a spy for Albania. She did not serve time in prison but was labeled a traitor and unable to find a job. (She fled to Slovenia shortly afterward.)

Yugoslavia had a few independent radio and TV stations, but their broadcasts were limited to urban areas. Meanwhile, Milosevic censored government-controlled television and radio broadcasts to ensure that they showed his government in the proper light and offered people only certain messages. Milosevic also used television and radio to fuel Serb nationalism. For instance, he saw to it that broadcasts were filled with insulting names for the Muslim and

Catholic majorities in Bosnia and Croatia. Even outlandish stories made the news. One report claimed that Bosnians were feeding Serb children to animals at the zoo in Sarajevo.

Actors and other artists were subject to strict censorship. Once, while taking bows during a curtain call, Serbian actor Voja Brajovic wore a T-shirt bearing the logo of a popular student-led group that opposed the Serbian government. The audience gave him a standing ovation that lasted fifteen minutes. The next day, the Serbian Ministry of Culture canceled Brajovic's play.

FRIENDS AND ENEMIES

Within Yugoslavia, Slobodan Milosevic was both adored and despised. Milosevic's strongest supporters were the large number of Serbs living throughout the nation. He spread the message of Serb nationalism that many of them wanted to hear, so they were unlikely to speak out against him. Even when Milosevic's policies led Yugoslavia into war and economic chaos, many Serbs continued to support him.

Milosevic's public support decreased after he had been in office for a number of years, but many Yugoslavians seemed angrier at the foreign nations that they felt were intervening in Yugoslavia's affairs than they were at Milosevic. Milosevic was not a perfect leader in the eyes of his people, but international interference was even less popular.

Milosevic also had many opponents, and some of them dared to protest openly. In the 1990s, the feminist group Women in Black demonstrated regularly in Belgrade to protest the nation's wars. With NATO bombings, the group stopped their protests.

One of the largest and most popular antigovernment groups was Otpor (Resistance), a student-led, prodemocracy group formed at Belgrade University in 1998. At first the Milosevic administration tried to ignore the dissident group. Then it began arresting and beating group members, but Otpor's strength only grew. By 2000 it had more than twenty-five thousand members. During national elections that year, the group did not promote any particular candidate for office. It just tried to get citizens mobilized to vote Milosevic out of office. Yugoslavian police raided Otpor's Belgrade office just days before the election, but the group continued to operate.

This group of idealistic young people posed a new problem for Milosevic because it did not operate like typical Yugoslavian opposition parties. Often, opposition parties spent more time arguing among themselves than attacking Milosevic's government. But Otpor's approach was different. It covered Serbia with images of its organizational symbol—a clenched fist. It also used humor and sarcasm to point out the government's failings. In one instance, Otpor posted birthday cards for Milosevic throughout Serbia. The cards expressed the wish that Milosevic would spend his next birthday at The Hague, where accused war criminals are tried.

THOUSANDS OF STUDENTS march through downtown Belgrade in 1996 to demonstrate against Milosevic.

THE SECURITY APPARATUS

Groups such as Otpor took a big risk in criticizing the government, because people who openly supported changes to the country's political system could be arrested and sentenced to from one to ten years in prison. The government frequently arrested protesters, even those who demonstrated peacefully.

Controlling dissidents was a high priority for Milosevic and other Yugoslavian leaders—both to maintain order in society and to keep themselves in power. The government wanted to stop all threats to its control, preferably before they had the opportunity to do much damage.

The government's main tool in fighting dissidents was the State Security Service (known by the initials of its Serbo-Croatian name, SDB). The SDB monitored people engaged in peaceful actions, such as protests or publishing material critical of the government, as well as more violent dissidents who engaged in assassinations or terrorist acts. The SDB heavily targeted minority ethnic groups, especially Croats and Albanian Muslims who opposed Serb control.

Undercover agents from the SDB tried to build relationships with people who were known to be critical of the government. Agents often posed as allies and joined dissident organizations. The government even used citizens against one another by requiring that they report crimes of all kinds, including political crimes, to the SDB.

When SDB efforts at keeping subversives quiet were not sufficient, the national government could send out its fifteen-thousand-member People's Militia. This group used heavily armored tanks

SERBIAN POLICE BREAK UP A PROTEST OF ANTI-GOVERNMENT CITIZENS IN
Belgrade in 1999. Police often used force to stop demonstrations.

and helicopters to control crowds and put down riots. Another fifteen thousand troops were responsible for border control throughout Yugoslavia.

LAW AND ORDER

Milosevic made use of the Yugoslavian judicial system to keep people fearful and quiet. This system was rigged in favor of the government. For instance, police in Yugoslavia did not need a warrant to arrest someone for a political crime.

The police could make an arrest and hold a suspect for up to three days before seeking approval from a judge. A judge could decide to hold a prisoner for as long as three months without any formal charges, and the Supreme Court, the nation's highest court, could order a person held for three additional months without charges. According to Amnesty International, a human rights organization, it was not uncommon for Yugoslavian police to abuse prisoners physically or emotionally to force confessions from them.

The Office of the Federal Public Prosecutor was in charge of trying people accused of crimes. This office was part of the Federal Secretariat for Internal Affairs, the same organization that oversaw the SDB. Thus dissidents often did not get fair trials because their arrests and trials were controlled by the same national government department.

According to Amnesty International, Milosevic kept hundreds of political prisoners in Yugoslavia's federal prisons. The organization condemned these prisons for their inhumane conditions and poor treatment of prisoners. Even Yugoslavians who were not arrested for illegal political activities sometimes suffered for their opposition to the government. Milosevic could have their passports taken away or have them fired from their jobs.

EXILES

Some dissidents chose to live in exile, outside of Yugoslavia, rather than risk being arrested or killed for their antigovernment activities. In the mid-1970s, Zoran Djindic was still a college student when he fled to Germany after speaking out for political change in Yugoslavia. He was later able to return home, and he became Serbia's prime minister in 2001. (He was assassinated in 2003.)

Vuk Draskovic *(shown below in 2007)* led a political party called the Serbian Renewal Movement in the late 1990s. He was popular and charismatic, and many considered him a likely candidate to oppose Milosevic's reelection to the FRY presidency in 2000. Then Draskovic survived two different assassination attempts, and his party decided he shouldn't run for president. Rather than staying in Serbia and risking assassination, Draskovic waited out Milosevic's 2000 reelection campaign in the Montenegro town of Budva. He returned to Serbian politics in late 2002, after Milosevic had been imprisoned at The Hague. In 2006 Draskovic became Serbia's foreign minister.

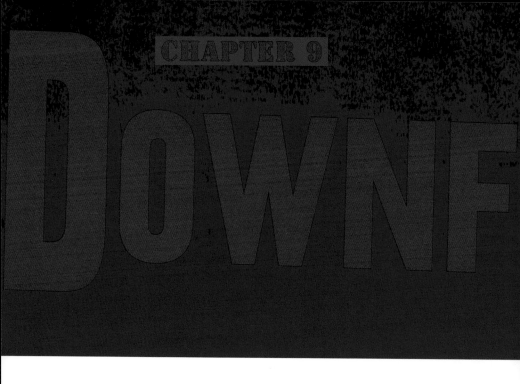

CHAPTER 9

WHEN THE CIVIL WARS IN YUGOSLAVIA were finally over, the international community directed its attention to the legacy of horror that had been left in the wake of the violence. The United Nations created the International Criminal Tribunal for the former Yugoslavia (ICTY) to try people accused of committing war crimes during the Yugoslavian wars. (As of 2009, more than 150 people have been charged with such crimes.)

On May 27, 1999, the ICTY formally charged Slobodan Milosevic with war crimes including genocide, crimes against humanity, and violations of the customs of war. He was president of Yugoslavia when the charges were filed and refused to turn himself over to the ICTY.

Slobodan Milosevic remained in power until October 2000, when he was voted out of office. At first, the Yugoslavian government refused to turn him over to the United Nations because

MILOSEVIC LEAVES A POLLING place in Belgrade during the 2000 Serbian elections. He was voted out of office that same year.

the country's constitution did not allow extradition (sending a person to another country to stand trial). However, the government held Milosevic on additional criminal charges, including stealing from the government treasury, corruption, and the murder of his former friend Ivan Stambolic.

After keeping Milosevic in prison in Belgrade, the Yugoslavian government gave in to international pressure and turned him over to the United Nations in 2001. Authorities secretly put him on a helicopter and whisked him out of the country in July. (Those who supported Milosevic argued that he had essentially been kidnapped because his removal from Yugoslavia was not in keeping with the country's laws.) On July 28, 2001, Milosevic arrived at the UN's International Court of Justice at The Hague, Netherlands.

ON TRIAL

The war crimes trial against Slobodan Milosevic began at The Hague on February 12, 2002. The ICTY decided to deal with Milosevic's role in three different conflicts—Bosnia-Herzegovina, Croatia, and Kosovo—in one war crimes trial.

MILOSEVIC SITS BETWEEN TWO GUARDS ON THE THIRD DAY OF HIS TRIAL at The Hague on February 14, 2002.

The indictment, or written statement of charges, said that in Bosnia-Herzegovina, Milosevic had been responsible for the killing of thousands of Bosnian Muslims and Croats, including the July 1995 massacre of thousands of Bosnian men and boys at Srebrenica. The indictment also said that Milosevic had a hand in the imprisonment and mistreatment of thousands of additional Bosnian Muslims and Croats, including women and the elderly.

In Croatia, Milosevic's crimes were listed as the murder of hundreds of civilians and the expulsion of hundreds of thousands of other civilians from their homes. The indictment said that Milosevic had collaborated with the Yugoslavian army and Serb paramilitary groups in carrying out these acts, by providing financial, material, and logistical support to their efforts. In the final conflict, Kosovo, Milosevic (and four of his colleagues) was charged with removing about eight hundred thousand Albanian Kosovars from their homes, the murder of hundreds, and widespread rape carried out by Serb soldiers.

Milosevic, trained as a lawyer at the University of Belgrade, chose to represent himself at the trial. The judge overseeing the case was Richard May, a former British lawyer. The chief prosecutor, the lawyer responsible for pursuing formal charges against Milosevic, was Swiss-born Carla Del Ponte.

From the start, Milosevic was belligerent and uncooperative with the court. He argued with the judge. He denounced the court as illegitimate, or illegal, and said that his arrest had been unlawful. He refused to enter a plea of guilty or not guilty so the court entered a not guilty plea on his behalf. The court also appointed two lawyers to help defend Milosevic, but he refused to meet with them.

When the trial began, the prosecution presented witness after witness. The first of many victims to testify, Agim Zeqiri described

MILOSEVIC SPEAKS DURING HIS TRIAL AT THE HAGUE IN 2004. MILOSEVIC
defended himself at the United Nations tribunal against war crimes charges.

how Milosevic's soldiers had burned down his village in Kosovo in March 1999 and killed sixteen members of his family. Another Kosovar described Serb troops massacring villagers in his town and blowing up the village mosque (Islamic house of worship). Many female rape victims testified in secret to protect their privacy and identities. They described fleeing their homes to escape from Serb armies, only to be captured and raped by Serb soldiers. Other witnesses told of Serb forces raining down shells on defenseless Kosovar villages, leaving them in flames. The litany of horrors went on like this day after day.

In the face of this overwhelming evidence, Milosevic remained defiant. He harassed witnesses who testified against him, calling them liars and pawns of the West. He said that massacre scenes had been staged, or faked. He blamed NATO bombs for most of the deaths in Kosovo. He also argued that many of the victims of Serb forces had not been civilians but instead were armed fighters.

Milosevic was in poor health when the trial began. He suffered from heart disease and high blood pressure and repeatedly said that he was too sick or too tired to appear in court, leading to delays that frustrated the prosecution.

The first phase of the trial dealt with events of the Kosovo War. Prosecutors then turned to earlier incidents in Croatia and Bosnia. Witnesses such as Yugoslavian political leaders and NATO commanders described how Milosevic had had ultimate knowledge of and control over atrocities such as the Srebrenica massacre. As before, Milosevic was defiant. He denied that his soldiers had committed any crimes. He even said that the Srebrenica massacre had been orchestrated by the West to make Serbs look bad.

After 293 days of trial stretching over two years, the prosecution rested its case. In all, nearly three hundred witnesses had testified for the prosecution. The prosecution had also submitted twenty-nine thousand pages of written evidence.

FADE OUT

With the prosecution rested, it was Milosevic's turn to present his defense, scheduled to begin on July 5, 2004. But when that date arrived, Milosevic was too ill to proceed. On August 31, he finally returned to court, where he presented the opening statement in his defense. In this statement, he denounced the accusations against him. He blamed NATO and the West for the wars in the former Yugoslavia and insisted that Serbs had been the victims, not the aggressors, in those wars. He announced that in the following months he would call more than sixteen hundred witnesses to testify in his defense, including former U.S. president Bill Clinton and then British prime minister Tony Blair. By this time, a new judge, Patrick Robinson, presided over the case.

The following months were marked by controversy and delays. Milosevic's health continued to decline. He refused to allow his court-appointed lawyers to take over the defense on his behalf. The defense proceeded in fits and starts

MILOSEVIC BEGAN HIS DEFENSE at his trial at The Hague in 2004. He is shown here in court in July 2004.

throughout 2005 and early 2006, and the star witnesses did not appear. At one point, Milosevic asked to travel to Russia—where his wife and son were then living—for medical treatment. The court refused his request, asserting that his UN-administered medical care was satisfactory.

The long-drawn-out trial took a turn for the bizarre in early 2006 when blood tests revealed the presence of an unprescribed medication in Milosevic's body. Milosevic and his supporters claimed that this drug was poison, administered by the authorities to kill him. His opponents charged that Milosevic had taken the drug himself to further damage his health and advance his case for going to Russia.

This medical controversy was ongoing when Milosevic was found dead in his prison cell on March 11, 2006. An autopsy showed that he had died from a heart attack (although some supporters continued to insist that he had been poisoned). On March 14, Judge Patrick Robinson formally closed the Milosevic trial without a verdict. He said that he regretted that Milosevic's victims would never see justice done.

Slobodan Milosevic was dead at the age of sixty-four. His support in Serbia once widespread was by then quite small. Serbia's greatly diminished Socialist Party organized a small funeral and had him buried in his hometown of Pozarevac. His wife and children could not return from abroad for the funeral, because they were wanted in Serbia on criminal charges. Most Serbians ignored the funeral.

MOURNERS ATTEND THE FUNERAL OF MILOSEVIC IN HIS HOMETOWN OF Pozarevac, near Belgrade, on March 18, 2006.

Slobodan Milosevic takes his place in history books among the brutal dictators of the twentieth century. The exact number who died during the wars in Yugoslavia is not known, but estimates put it at 250,000. Many millions survived the wars but endured horrors such as imprisonment, rape, and the destruction of their homes.

When Milosevic died in March 2006, the London-based *Economist* magazine wrote a scathing obituary, accusing him of plundering the Serbian and Yugoslavian treasuries, associating with murderers, fostering war, and encouraging ethnic cleansing. The obituary concluded by calling Milosevic a monster. Many would agree with this assessment.

INTO THE EU?

In 2007 Serbia sought entry to the European Union (EU), a political and economic union of member nations. However, Serbia has a record of human rights abuses in its homes for the disabled, and this record is a serious setback for Serbia's EU application. All EU member countries must have proven dedication to citizens' rights, and the practice of locking away sufferers of disabilities is not acceptable to the EU community. Serbia's new constitution guarantees rights to all citizens, but that guarantee is of little value when thousands of disabled children and adults remain tied to their beds with no realistic hope of release. Croatia, Bosnia-Herzegovina, Macedonia, and Montenegro have also applied for EU membership. To be accepted for membership, these nations must show that they have democratic governments, with freedom of religion, human rights protections, a free press, and other democratic institutions. Slovenia became an EU member in 2004.

MOVING FORWARD

In 2009, ten years after the Kosovo War ended, Yugoslavia can no longer be found on a map of the world. The country that used to consist of six republics and two provinces has been fractured. Yugoslavia officially ceased to exist in 2003, when its two remaining republics, Serbia and Montenegro, changed their name from the Federal Republic of Yugoslavia to the Union of Serbia and Montenegro. Within three years, that union too dissolved. On May 21, 2006, the citizens of Montenegro voted to become an independent nation.

MONTENEGRINS STAND IN LINE WAITING TO VOTE ON MAY 21, 2006.

In that election, citizens voted to become an independent nation. Not long after, all the republics that had made up Yugoslavia were governing themselves.

The question on the ballot read, "Do you want the Republic of Montenegro to be an independent state with full international and legal subjectivity [status]?" Serbia and Montenegro had agreed that Montenegro would become independent only if at least 55 percent of voters supported the move. When the votes were tallied, 55.4 percent supported independence. The split with Serbia became official on June 5, 2006.

Within Serbia, the province of Kosovo continues to call for independence. It declared itself an independent nation in February 2008, but the international community has not recognized its independent status.

AGIM ÇEKU *(CENTER)*, **WHO SERVED AS PRIME MINISTER OF KOSOVO FROM** 2006 to 2008, has worked to make peace between Kosovar Serbs and Albanian Muslims as they rebuild Kosovo. He is shown here in 2006.

One of the difficulties in the struggle for an independent Kosovo is that not all countries around the world support it. The United States and most European nations do, but Russia is opposed, based on its long history of political alliance with Serbia. In newly independent nations, the majority population often ends up oppressing the minority, and in the case of an independent Kosovo, the majority ethnic Albanians might target the minority Serbs. In addition, the international community might have to bear the significant costs associated with helping a small new country establish its own

NEW ALLIES

Since the end of the Kosovo War, many Islamic groups from the Middle East and elsewhere have provided desperately needed aid to Kosovo's Muslim people. Saudi Arabia has provided funds to rebuild mosques that were damaged or destroyed during the fighting. Muslim charities have given scholarships that enable young Albanian Muslims to study in the Middle East.

Students who accept the scholarships are often changed by their experiences in the Middle East. It is not unusual for scholarship students to return home wearing traditional Muslim clothing, including hijabs (head scarves) for women. The students often become more devout Muslims than those who do not leave the country for schooling. These changes concern some Kosovars, who fear that the young people's fundamentalist Islamic behavior might scare off Kosovo's Western allies, including the United States.

government and economy, since Kosovo could not afford them on its own. This aid would likely have to come from the United Nations and the European Union, and these groups aren't eager to take on these costs.

Richard Holbrooke was President Clinton's special envoy to Kosovo during the late 1990s. He believes that Kosovo's independence might lead to renewed warfare, since the Serbs still don't want to let the province go. In a 2007 *New Yorker* article,

LAND MINES

A decade after the end of Yugoslavia's civil wars, the country's former republics are still cleaning up the mess. One of the lingering dangers is land mines. These bombs were planted in the ground during the wars of the 1990s. When the fighting stopped, many of them remained. Modern-day Serbia still contains one of the highest numbers of land mines in all of Europe. These bombs still kill and maim civilians. Efforts continue to remove the mines, but funding is scarce and progress is slow.

The international community has called for a ban on these brutal weapons, which can kill anyone who steps on them, whether they are allies or enemies, adults or children. In 2003 Serbia and Montenegro added their names to an international treaty to ban land mines.

Holbrooke said, "The chances of violence are very high here." Holbrooke went on to describe the situation as "a fast-approaching diplomatic train wreck."

The roots of anger, mistrust, and violence in the former Yugoslavia stem from history, religious differences, and nationalism. Slobodan Milosevic was a prominent and unforgettable figure in the historic and brutally violent struggle that erupted in the nation he led in the 1990s. As newly independent nations emerge from the former Yugoslavia, only time will tell if their citizens can heal the wounds left in the wake of that struggle.

WHO'S WHO?

DRAGOSLAV AVRAMOVIC (1914–2001): Avramovic was born in Skopje, Macedonia. He became an economist and worked in Yugoslavia and later at the World Bank, an international lending organization. Milosevic appointed Avramovic to head the Yugoslavian National Bank in 1994. Avramovic tried to control inflation by stopping the printing of money to fund Yugoslavia's wars. He also supported some market-based economic reforms to the country's old Communist system. He managed to quickly get the inflation rate down to reasonable levels, which made him popular with the people. But Milosevic did not support Avramovic's changes and dismissed him from his position in 1996.

AGIM CEKU (B. 1960): Ceku, an Albanian Muslim, began his military career in the Yugoslavian People's Army (YPA). He deserted the army in 1991 and began to fight against YPA soldiers during Croatia's struggle for independence. In May 1999, he became chief of staff of the Kosovo Liberation Army (KLA). Under his leadership, the KLA went from a disorganized guerrilla group to a disciplined military organization. Serbia insists that Ceku is a war criminal, but the International Criminal Tribunal for the former Yugoslavia (ICTY) never formally charged him with any crimes. He became prime minister of Kosovo in 2006 and served until 2008.

ZORAN DJINDIC (1952–2003): A lifelong opponent of Communism, Djindic angered the Yugoslavian Communist Party by pushing for a new political direction for Yugoslavia. He fled to Germany, where he completed a doctoral degree in philosophy. After returning to Yugoslavia, he took a teaching position at a Yugoslavian university and helped found a liberal political party. In 1990 he won a seat in Serbia's legislature. Later in his career, Djindic led a coalition of political parties called the Democratic Opposition of Serbia (DOS). DOS candidates won a large majority of seats in the Yugoslavian legislature in 2000. The DOS victory was a final decisive defeat for Slobodan Milosevic and his Communist Party colleagues.

RAMUSH HARADINAJ (B. 1968): An Albanian KLA leader during the Kosovo War, Haradinaj briefly served as Kosovo's prime minister in late 2004 and early 2005 before being indicted for war crimes by the ICTY. The ICTY charged that Haradinaj was responsible for the killing of civilians during the war. When the ICTY issued its charges against him in 2005, Haradinaj resigned his post as prime minister and flew to The Hague. He was found not guilty on April 3, 2008, due to a lack of evidence against him.

PETER KARAGEORGE (1844–1921): Karageorge was descended from a famous Serbian hero who had rebelled against the Ottoman Empire in the early 1800s. In 1903 Karageorge became the king of Serbia. He had been educated in France, and when he took the reins in Serbia, he strove to create a Western-style monarchy based on the authority of a constitution. When Serbia became part of the Kingdom of Serbs, Croats, and Slovenes, Peter became the new nation's first king. He served for only three years before dying. He left the throne to his son Alexander.

ANTE MARKOVIC (B. 1924): Markovic was prime minister of Yugoslavia's national government from March 1989 to December 1991. He supported a market-based economic system designed to help ease Yugoslavia's economic difficulties. He also fought for democratic reforms to the nation's political system. He was briefly the most popular politician in the country, but Slobodan Milosevic attacked him, charging that he supported Western-style democracy and opposed Serb causes and Communism. After losing support of the Yugoslavian army, Markovic resigned as prime minister in December 1991 and entered the business world. Markovic testified against Milosevic at Milosevic's war crimes trial.

MIRJANA MARKOVIC (B. 1942): Markovic was born in Serbia during World War II. Her mother was a member of the Yugoslavian resistance forces and was captured by the Germans, so Markovic was raised by her grandmother. She met Slobodan Milosevic when they were in high school together, and they married in 1965. A sociologist at the University of Belgrade, Markovic was a vital part of Milosevic's political career. Insiders who were close to the couple said that he relied heavily upon her ideas and trusted her above any other aides or advisers. She was a staunch Communist who was unpopular with many Serbs and members of the foreign press. She currently lives in exile in Russia and is wanted in Serbia on charges of fraud and ordering the murder of a journalist.

SLOBODAN MILOSEVIC (1941–2006): A staunch Communist, Milosevic climbed his way through the ranks of Yugoslavia's Communist Party. He served as president of the republic of Serbia from 1989 to 1997 and as president of Yugoslavia from 1997 to 2000. During his time in office, Yugoslavia suffered through three civil wars, international economic sanctions, and the secession of four of the country's original six republics. The ICTY charged Milosevic with war crimes for his actions during Yugoslavia's war. He died in prison while his trial was still in progress, never having been convicted or found not guilty.

ZELJKO RAZNJATOVIC (1952–2000): Raznjatovic, known as Arkan, began his career in a secret police force run by Yugoslavian president Josip Broz Tito. He worked undercover in Western Europe, where his job was to assassinate Tito's political opponents who had fled Yugoslavia. Arkan returned to Yugoslavia after Tito's death. In 1990 Milosevic chose him to head the Serbian Volunteer Guard, a paramilitary group. He fought in the Kosovo War and allegedly committed a variety of war crimes. The ICTY indicted him, but he was assassinated in 2000, before standing trial. His murderer has not been caught.

IVAN STAMBOLIC (1936–2000): Stambolic was a Serb and close friend of Slobodan Milosevic from their days as students at the University of Belgrade Law School. Powerful political connections, particularly his uncle Peter Stambolic, helped propel his political career. In turn, Stambolic helped advance Milosevic's political career. Stambolic became president of Serbia in 1985. In 1987 Milosevic turned on his friend. He began a smear campaign that resulted in Stambolic being voted out of office. Milosevic then replaced Stambolic as the Serbian president. On August 25, 2000, Stambolic disappeared. His body was later found, and in 2005, a court ruled that Milosevic had ordered his assassination.

JOSIP BROZ TITO (1892–1980): Born in Croatia, Tito became a Communist after World War I and helped form the Yugoslavian Communist Party. King Alexander outlawed the party and had Tito jailed for his political work. During World War II, Tito led Communist resistance forces fighting the German occupation of Yugoslavia. He became president of Yugoslavia in 1945. Under Tito's style of Communism, known as Titoism, Yugoslavia developed a fairly healthy economy. Tito was also able to hold the nation together, despite its many ethnic and religious divisions.

TIMELINE

600s   Slavic people take control of the Balkans.

800s   Many Slavic peoples in the Balkans convert to Christianity.

1054   The Christian Church splits into two halves: Eastern Orthodox Christianity and Roman Catholicism. Many Slavic people affiliate with one or the other of these churches.

1300s   The Ottoman Empire invades the Balkans. The Ottomans spread the Islamic religion to the region.

1912   Serbia, Montenegro, Greece, and Bulgaria create the Balkan League for defense against the Ottoman Empire. The league defeats the Ottomans in the First Balkan War.

1913   Bulgaria fights against Romania, Greece, Serbia, and the Ottomans in the Second Balkan War.

1914   World War I begins when a Serbian assassinates Archduke Franz Ferdinand of Austria-Hungary.

1918   World War I ends. The Kingdom of Serbs, Croats, and Slovenes becomes an independent state.

1929   King Alexander seizes control of the Kingdom of Serbs, Croats, and Slovenes. He renames the kingdom Yugoslavia.

1939   World War II begins when Germany invades Poland.

1941   The Axis powers invade Yugoslavia. Many Yugoslavians resist the occupying forces. Slobodan Milosevic is born in a small town in eastern Serbia called Pozarevac.

1945   Josip Broz Tito becomes the leader of Yugoslavia. He bases his government on the principles of Socialism.

1963   Tito declares himself Yugoslavia's president for life.

1964 Slobodan Milosevic graduates from the University of Belgrade Law School.

1974 Tito creates a new constitution to strengthen Yugoslavia's central government.

1980 Tito dies, leaving behind the 1974 constitution to help guide the government.

1986 Milosevic becomes the leader of the Communist Party of Serbia. Ivan Stambolic becomes president of Serbia.

1989 Milosevic becomes president of Serbia. The Communist governments of Eastern Europe begin to disintegrate.

1990 The League of Communists of Yugoslavia holds its Fourteenth Congress. The meeting soon breaks up when the Slovenian and Croatian delegates leave in protest. Slovenia and Croatia hold multiparty elections.

1991 Slovenia, Croatia, and Macedonia break away from the rest of Yugoslavia.

1992 War begins in Bosnia-Herzegovina after its citizens vote for independence from Yugoslavia. The international community enacts a trade embargo against Serbia.

1993 The Bosnian Serbs reject the United Nation's Vance-Owen Plan for Bosnian peace.

1995 The United States negotiates the Dayton Accord, which ends the fighting between warring ethnic groups in Bosnia-Herzegovina.

1996 Serbia and Montenegro establish a new state called the Federal Republic of Yugoslavia (FRY).

1997 Milosevic is elected president of FRY. Fighting begins between the Kosovo Liberation Army and FRY troops.

1999 NATO begins bombing raids in Serbia and Kosovo to end the Kosovo War. The International Criminal Tribunal for the former Yugoslavia charges Milosevic with war crimes.

2000 Slobodan Milosevic loses the presidential election and resigns as president of Yugoslavia.

2001 The United Nations arrests Milosevic and takes him to the International Court of Justice at The Hague, Netherlands.

2002 Milosevic's war crimes trial begins. He chooses to represent himself in the trial.

2003 Yugoslavia ceases to exist as a nation when FRY changes its name to the Union of Serbia and Montenegro.

2006 Milosevic is found dead in his cell at The Hague, with his war crimes trial still unfinished. Serbia and Montenegro split into two separate nations.

2007 Serbia applies for membership in the European Union.

2008 Kosovo declares its independence from Serbia, but the international community does not recognize its independence.

2009 Ethnic violence flares up in Kosovo. Radovan Karadzic's war crimes trial begins at The Hague.

GLOSSARY

capitalism: an economic system featuring private ownership of business and property, business competition, and little government involvement in business operations

civilians: people who are not members of military forces

civil war: a war between opposing groups of citizens in the same country

commune: In Yugoslavia, small groups of workers who oversaw matters of local governance and economic activity

Communism: in theory, a social system in which government is not necessary, everyone works according to his or her abilities, and the society produces enough goods to supply everyone's needs. Communism as practiced in Yugoslavia, the Soviet Union, and other nations was actually Socialism, a system in which the government owns and controls most business, property, and economic activity.

democracy: a nation in which citizens control the government by voting for lawmakers and other government officials. Most democracies guarantee people freedom of speech, freedom of religion, and other basic rights.

dictator: a leader who rules with absolute power and usually rules oppressively

dissident: someone who disagrees with the established political system

embargo: cutting off trade with a country in an attempt to damage its economy and force its leaders to change policies

ethnic cleansing: the expulsion, imprisonment, or killing of an ethnic minority by an ethnic majority to achieve ethnic sameness throughout a region

extradition: the surrender of an alleged criminal by one authority (such as a government) to another

genocide: the deliberate and systematic mistreatment and killing of a national, political, religious, cultural, or racial group

inflation: a situation in which the value of a country's money declines sharply while the prices of goods jump

Islam: a major world religion. People who practice Islam are called Muslims. The prophet Muhammad founded the Islamic religion on the Arabian Peninsula in the A.D. 600s.

nationalism: a philosophy that emphasizes loyalty to one's own ethnic group or nation above all else

refugee: a person who flees his or her country to escape danger or persecution

sanctions: economic restrictions imposed by nations and intended to pressure other governments to make changes

secede: to withdraw from an organization, such as a political federation

Socialism: a political and economic system in which the government controls the economy, with little private property or private business

terrorism: the use of violence to create fear, usually for political purposes

Titoism: Yugoslavia's system of Communism under President Josip Broz Tito. Tito's system put some economic control in the hands of people at local levels, rather than centralizing it at the national government level as was done in the Soviet Union and other Communist nations.

war crimes: military violations of the rules of warfare, such as killing civilians

West: the industrialized, democratic nations of North America and Europe

YUGOSLAVIAN AND INTERNATIONAL ORGANIZATIONS

EU—European Union: a group made up primarily of European nations that cooperate on economic and diplomatic matters. The EU intervened several times in the Yugoslavian wars. In the 2000s, Slovenia became an EU member and several other former Yugoslavian republics have applied for membership.

FEC—Federal Executive Council: a group that developed ideas for new laws in Yugoslavia. The FEC consisted of the heads of the country's twelve major government departments, as well as a prime minister, two deputy prime ministers, and other representatives.

FRY—Federal Republic of Yugoslavia: the new name for Yugoslavia after the republics of Slovenia, Croatia, Bosnia-Herzegovinia, and Macedonia broke away in the 1990s. The new Yugoslavia consisted of only Serbia and Montenegro.

ICTY—International Criminal Tribunal for the former Yugoslavia: a court assembled by the United Nations to prosecute those charged with committing human rights abuses during the civil wars within the former Yugoslavia.

KLA—Kosovo Liberation Army: a fighting force formed in Kosovo to oppose the Yugoslavian People's Army. The organization's goal was to secure independence for the province of Kosovo and its majority of ethnic Albanian citizens.

LCY—League of Communists of Yugoslavia: the only legal political party in Yugoslavia from 1946 until 1990. In addition to the national party, each republic and province had its own branch of the party, such as the League of Communists of Serbia. The national party broke up at its Fourteenth Congress in 1990, although some of the regional organizations continued to operate under new names.

NATO—North Atlantic Treaty Organization: an international organization formed after World War II to provide military protection to member nations and to provide international peacekeeping. The member countries are primarily European but also include the United States and Canada.

SAWPY—Socialist Alliance of Working People of Yugoslavia: a large political organization, with millions of Yugoslavian members. Controlled by the LCY, SAWPY involved citizens in government and the Communist Party at the local level.

SDB—State Security Services: SDB stood for Sluzba Drzavne Bezbednosti, which means "State Security Services" in Serbo-Croatian. This group was responsible for maintaining Communist control in Yugoslavia by infiltrating dissident groups and spying on and arresting dissidents.

UN—United Nations: an organization of nations formed after World War II to work together for world peace and the betterment of humanity. The United Nations sent peacekeeping troops to Yugoslavia during the Yugoslavian wars and also convened the ICTY to try individuals charged with committing war crimes during those conflicts.

YPA—Yugoslavian People's Army: Yugoslavia's national army

PRONUNCIATION GUIDE
Bosnia-Herzegovina: BAWZ-nee-uh HEHRT-seh-gaw-vee-nah

Kosovo: KAW-saw-voh

Milosevic: muh-LOH-suh-vihch

Montenegro: mawn-tay-NAY-groh

Pozarevac: poh-ZHAHR-uh-vahts

Sarajevo: sah-rah-YEH-voh

Vojvodina: VOY-vaw-dee-nah

Yugoslavia: yoo-goh-SLAH-vee-uh

SOURCE NOTES

19 Dusko Doder and Louise Branson, *Milosevic: Portrait of a Tyrant* (New York: Free Press, 1999), 14.

42 Leslie Benson, *Yugoslavia: A Concise History* (New York: Palgrave Publishing, 2001), 137.

45 Ibid., 149.

69 Doder and Branson, *Milosevic*, 225.

75 Ibid., 142.

77 William Finnegan, "The Countdown: The Disputed Region Gears Up to Declare War," *New Yorker*, October 15, 2007, 73.

79 Richard J. Newman, "In the Skies over Serbia," *US News and World Report*, May 24, 1999, 24–25.

91 Mental Disability Rights International, *Torment Not Treatment: Serbia's Segregation and Abuse of Children and Adults with Disabilities* (Washington, DC: Mental Disability Rights International, 2007), 16.

122 Alison Behnke, *Serbia and Montenegro in Pictures* (Minneapolis: Twenty-First Century Books, 2007), 34.

125 Finnegan, "Countdown," 72.

SELECTED BIBLIOGRAPHY

Benson, Leslie. *Yugoslavia: A Concise History*. New York: Palgrave
    Publishing, 2001.

Curtis, Glenn E., ed. *Yugoslavia: A Country Study*. 3rd ed. Washington, DC:
    Library of Congress Federal Research Division, 1992.

Doder, Dusko, and Louise Branson. *Milosevic: Portrait of a Tyrant*. New York:
    Free Press, 1999.

Finnigan, William. "The Countdown: The Disputed Region Gears Up to
    Declare War." *New Yorker*, October 15, 2007, 70–79.

Johnstone, Diana. *Fool's Crusade*. New York: Monthly Review Press, 2003.

Laughland, John. *Travesty: The Trial of Slobodan Milosevic and the
    Corruption of International Justice*. Ann Arbor, MI: Pluto Press, 2007.

Magstadt, Thomas M., *Nations and Governments: Comparative Politics in
    Regional Perspective*. 5th ed. Belmont, CA: Wadsworth, 2005.

Mental Disability Rights International. *Torment Not Treatment: Serbia's
    Segregation and Abuse of Children and Adults with Disabilities*.
    Washington, DC: Mental Disability Rights International, 2007.

Newman, Richard J. "In the Skies over Serbia." *US News and World Report*,
    May 24, 1999, 24–25.

Stevanovic, Vidosav, and Trude Johansson. *Milosevic: The People's Tyrant*.
    New York: I. B. Tauris, 2004.

FURTHER READING AND WEBSITES

Andryszewski, Tricia. *Kosovo: The Splintering of Yugoslavia*. Brookfield, CT: Millbrook Press, 2000. This book presents the Kosovo conflict in an easy-to-understand format. Photographs and eyewitness quotations help bring the situation into focus.

Benhke, Alison. *Serbia and Montenegro in Pictures*. Minneapolis: Twenty-First Century Books, 2007. Serbia and Montenegro were formerly Yugoslavian republics and were briefly one nation before Montenegro declared its independence in 2006. This book examines the history, geography, culture, and society of both regions.

Englar, Mary. *Bosnia-Herzegovina in Pictures*. Minneapolis: Twenty-First Century Books, 2006. In 1992 Bosnia-Herzegovina declared its independence from Yugoslavia—and found itself embroiled in a brutal war. This book for young readers explores modern Bosnia-Herzegovina as well as its history.

January, Brendan. *Genocide: Modern Crimes against Humanity*. Minneapolis: Twenty-First Century Books, 2006. This title examines genocide in the modern era, with one chapter devoted to crimes against humanity in Bosnia.

Marcovitz, Hal. *The Balkans: People in Conflict*. Philadelphia: Chelsea House Publications, 2002. This book for young readers sheds light on the complexity of the former Yugoslavia, its various civil wars, and leaders such as Slobodan Milosevic.

Mead, Alice. *Girl of Kosovo*. New York: Farrar, Straus and Giroux, 2001. This novel for young readers tells the story of Zana, an eleven-year-old ethnic Albanian girl in Kosovo. Caught in the horror of the Kosovo War, Zana tries not to succumb to the despair and hatred she sees around her.

WEBSITES

International Criminal Tribunal for the Former Yugoslavia

> http://www.un.org/icty/
>
> This website offers detailed information on Yugoslavian war crimes trials, including courtroom audio and video.

Milosevic's Yugoslavia

> http://news.bbc.co.uk/hi/english/static/in_depth/europe/2000/milosevic_yugoslavia/default.stm
>
> Created by the British Broadcasting Corporation (BBC), this website offers an in-depth look at Milosevic and the Yugoslavian wars.

vgsbooks.com

> http://www.vgsbooks.com
>
> This home page for Lerner Publishing Group's Visual Geography Series® provides links to online information, including geographical, historical, demographic, cultural, and economic websites, as well as late-breaking news, for 96 countries.

INDEX

INDEX

PHOTO ACKNOWLEDGMENTS

The images in this book are used with the permission of: AP Photo/Srdjan Ilic, pp. 1, 45, 60, 74, 103, 113; © Paul Vreeker/AFP/Getty Images, p. 7; AP Photo/ Mikica Petrovic, pp. 8, 109; © Gilbert M. Grosvenor/National Geographic/ Getty Images, p. 11; © Mansell/Time & Life Pictures/Getty Images, p. 13; © Laura Westlund/Independent Picture Service, pp. 16, 24; © Evening Standard/ Hulton Archive/Getty Images, p. 17; AP Photo, pp. 18, 41, 53, 66; © John Phillips/ Time & Life Pictures/Getty Images, p. 23; © Chris Ware/Keystone Features/ Hulton Archive/Getty Images, p. 26; AP Photo/Max Desfor, p. 29; AP Photo/ Matija Kokovic, p. 39; AP Photo/Martin Cleaver, p. 47; © Gerald Malie/AFP/ Getty Images, p. 48; © Bettmann/CORBIS, p. 50; AP Photo/Dusan Vranic, pp. 55, 101; AP Photo/Dragan Filipovic, p. 57; AP Photo/Ron Haviv/VII, p. 63; AP Photo/ Rikard Larma, p. 67; © Cynthia Johnson/Time & Life Pictures/Getty Images, p. 69; AP Photo/David Brauchli, pp. 76, 107; AP Photo/Santiago Lyon, p. 77; AP Photo/Visar Kryeziu, pp. 78, 96; AP Photo/Darko Vojinovic, pp. 81, 121; © Barca Nadezdic/Newsmakers/Getty Images, p. 82; © Tibor Bognar/Art Directors & TRIP, p. 85; © Mohsen Rastani/Art Directors & TRIP, p. 86; © NATO/Getty Images, p. 88; AP Photo/Pier Paolo Cito, p. 90; © Docevoc Velimir/Art Directors & TRIP, pp. 95 (left), 97; © age fotostock/SuperStock, p. 95 (right); © Frederick Florin/AFP/Getty Images, p. 111; © Robin Utrecht/AFP/Getty Images, p. 114; AP Photo/ICTY, via APTN, p. 116; © Michel Porro/Getty Images, p. 118; AP Photo/Louisa Gouliamaki, Pool, p. 119; AP Photo/Boris Grdanoski, p. 122.

Front Cover: © Michel Porro/Getty Images; AP Photo/David Brauchli (background).

AUTHOR BIOGRAPHY

Kimberly L. Sullivan holds a PhD in political science and has been a college instructor for more than ten years. In addition to writing nonfiction, she has also published a fantasy novel for young adults. Sullivan also wrote *Muammar al-Qaddafi's Libya* for the Dictatorships series. A lifelong Illinois resident, she lives in the Chicago suburbs with her husband and son.